Waldo Selden Pratt

Songs of Worship for the Sunday-School

Waldo Selden Pratt

Songs of Worship for the Sunday-School

ISBN/EAN: 9783337290184

Printed in Europe, USA, Canada, Australia, Japan

Cover: Foto ©Thomas Meinert / pixelio.de

More available books at **www.hansebooks.com**

SONGS OF WORSHIP

FOR THE SUNDAY-SCHOOL

EDITED BY

WALDO S. PRATT

NEW-YORK
THE CENTURY CO.

INTRODUCTORY NOTE.

THESE SONGS OF WORSHIP are intended to form a compact manual of musical worship, suitable for the Sunday School or for other church services. The hymns have been chosen so as to afford expression for all the principal forms of devout approach to God. Descriptive, hortatory, and didactic poems are almost entirely omitted. It is hoped that the classification, though obviously only a suggestion, will conduce to an intelligent use of the hymns as direct utterances of worship.

The tunes are meant to be genuine and dignified embodiments of the dominant sentiment of the various hymns. Triviality and mere jingle are avoided, simply because they express nothing. Many tunes were written specially for the book, and all have been chosen and arranged with reference to practical utility.

This collection is intended to serve as an introduction to the use of any of the leading church hymnals, and to be a real educator of taste in church music. It is large enough to afford variety for a series of years, and high enough in poetic and musical standard to justify careful and progressive study.

The editor will be well repaid for his labor upon these SONGS if they shall contribute to the wider appreciation and use of our nobler hymns and tunes as among the choicest means of publicly worshiping God.

WALDO S. PRATT.

HARTFORD THEOLOGICAL SEMINARY,
   October 1, 1887.

CONTENTS.

SONGS OF THE LORD'S DAY ...... 1 — 29

    THE DAY .... 1 — 5
    MORNING .... 6 — 13
    EVENING .... 14 — 29

SONGS OF THE LORD'S HOUSE .. 30 — 56

    OPENING OF SERVICE .... 30 — 40
    SINGING .... 41 — 43
    THE WORD .... 44 — 50
    CLOSE OF SERVICE .... 51 — 56

SONGS OF ADORATION .... 57 — 91

    TO THE FATHER AND TO THE
        TRINITY .... 57 — 70
    TO CHRIST .... 71 — 89
    GLORIAS .... 90 — 91

SONGS OF THANKSGIVING ..... 92 — 104

SONGS TO THE HOLY SPIRIT 105 — 114

SONGS OF CONFESSION AND SUPPLICATION } 115 — 158

    CONFESSION .... 115 — 125
    SUPPLICATION FOR GRACE .... 126 — 139
    SUPPLICATION FOR GUIDANCE 140 — 158

SONGS OF TRUST AND CONSECRATION } .... 159 — 187

    TRUST .... 159 — 173
    CONSECRATION .... 174 — 187

SONGS OF WORK AND WARFARE 188 — 208

    WARFARE .... 188 — 200
    MISSIONS .... 201 — 208

SONGS OF HEAVEN .... 209 — 229

SONGS FOR SPECIAL DAYS ... 230 — 265

    CHRISTMAS .... 230 — 246
    NEW YEAR'S 247
    PALM SUNDAY 248
    THE CRUCIFIXION .... 249 — 250
    EASTER .... 251 — 260
    ASCENSION .... 261 — 265

PUBLISHERS' NOTE.

Attention is called to the fact that many of the tunes and musical arrangements in this book have been specially made for it and are the exclusive property of The Century Co. Some are inserted by permission of the owners, the Rev. E. P. Parker, D. D., Walter B. Gilbert, Mus. Doc., Messrs. E. and J. B. Young & Co., the Rev. C. L. Hutchins, and others. The chants are printed as in "Aids to Common Worship," issued by this company. All rights of republication are reserved and will be defended by the owners of the copyrights.

SONGS OF THE LORD'S DAY.

2. Jesus, we love to meet on this Thy holy Day.

THE LORD'S DAY.

Mrs. E. R. Parson, 1836.   "BEECHCROFT."   T. G. Reed, 1880?

1. Jesus, we love to meet on this Thy holy Day;
   We worship 'round Thy seat on this Thy holy Day.
   Thou tender, heav'nly Friend, to Thee our pray'rs ascend,

2. We dare not trifle now on this Thy holy Day;
   In silent awe we bow on this Thy holy Day.
   Check ev'ry wand'ring thought, and let us all be taught

3. We listen to Thy Word on this Thy holy Day;
   Bless all that we have heard on this Thy holy Day.
   Go with us when we part, and to each youthful heart

THE LORD'S DAY.

Jesus, we love to meet.—*Concluded.*

O'er our young spir - its bend, on this Thy ho - ly Day.
To serve Thee as we ought, on this Thy ho - ly Day.
Thy sav - ing grace im - part on this Thy ho - ly Day. A-MEN.

Blest Day of God, most calm, most bright.   3

J. MASON, 1683.   "MOUNT CALVARY."   R. STEWART, 1874.

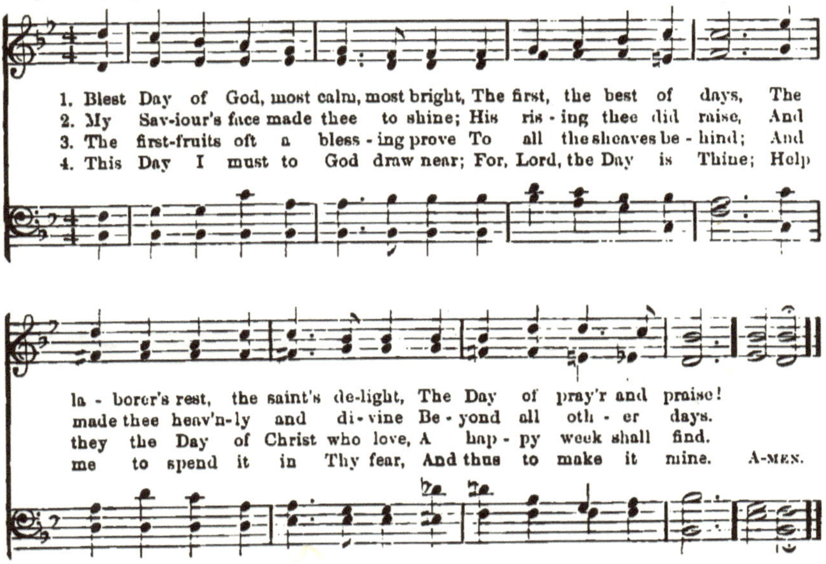

1. Blest Day of God, most calm, most bright, The first, the best of days, The
2. My Sav-iour's face made thee to shine; His ris - ing thee did raise, And
3. The first-fruits oft a bless - ing prove To all the sheaves be - hind; And
4. This Day I must to God draw near; For, Lord, the Day is Thine; Help

la - borer's rest, the saint's de-light, The Day of pray'r and praise!
made thee heav'n-ly and di - vine Be - yond all oth - er days.
they the Day of Christ who love, A hap - py week shall find.
me to spend it in Thy fear, And thus to make it mine. A-MEN.

THE LORD'S DAY.   5
Come, let us all with one accord.

H. M. C., 1872.   G. A. MACFARREN.
Allegro.

1. Come, let us all with one ac - cord A - dore and
2. That saw pri - me - val dark - ness break, And that more
3. Then on this day let us a - dore Our God, and

mag - ni - fy the Lord, And fes - tal ser - vice pay;
glo - rious life a - wake That last - eth ev - er - more;
sup - pli - ca - tions pour That, when worlds pass a - way,

On this the Day that God hath blest, The day of
That saw hell's le - gions pros - trate fall, And Christ, tri -
Thro' Christ's dear grace our souls may rest, In peace and

rit.

peace and heav'n - ly rest, The Lord's own ho - ly Day;—
umph - ant o - ver all, His own to heav'n re - store.
joy for ev - er blest Till the great Judg-ment - Day. A-MEN.

THE LORD'S DAY. MORNING.

Christ, whose glory fills the skies.—*Concluded.*

Sun of Right-eous-ness, a - rise, Tri-umph o'er the shades of night;

Day-spring from on high, be near; Day-star, in our hearts ap-pear! A-MEN.

This is the day of light.

7

J. ELLERTON, 1868.   "SWABIA."   German, 1745.

1. This is the day of light! Let there be light to - day! O Day-spring, rise up-
on our night, And chase its gloom a - way.
2. This is the day of rest! Our fail - ing strength re-new; On wea-ry brain and
troubl'd breast Shed Thou Thy fresh'ning dew.
3. This is the day of peace! Thy peace our spir - its fill! Bid Thou the blasts of
discord cease; The waves of strife be still. A-MEN.

4 This is the day of pray'r!
Let earth to heav'n draw near:
Lift up our hearts to seek Thee there;
Come down to meet us here.

5 This is the first of days:
Send forth Thy quick'ning breath,
And wake dead souls to love and praise,
O Vanquisher of Death! AMEN.

THE LORD'S DAY. MORNING.

The dawn of God's new Sabbath.—*Concluded.*

3 Yet still, O Lord long-suff'ring,
  Still grant us in our need
 Here in Thy holy presence
  The saving Name to plead:
 And on Thy day of blessings,
  Within Thy temple-walls.
 ‖: To foretaste the pure worship
  Of Zion's golden halls. :‖

4 Until in joy and gladness
  We reach that home at last,
 When life's short week of sorrow
  And sin and strife is past;
 When angel-hands have gather'd
  The first ripe fruit for Thee,
 ‖: O Father, Son, and Spirit,
  Most Holy Trinity! :‖ Amen.

Safely through another week. 9

J. NEWTON, 1779.   G. A. BURDETT, 1886.
Andante.

1. Safe - ly through an - oth - er week, God has brought us on our way;
2. Mer - cies mul - ti - plied each hour, Gra - cious Lord, our praise de - mand;
3. As Thy sun doth o'er us rise, May we feel Thy pres - ence near;

Let us now a bless-ing seek On this ho - ly Sab - bath day,
Guard-ed by Thy might-y pow'r, Nour-ish'd by Thy bounteous hand.
May Thy glo - ry meet our eyes, As we in Thy House ap - pear.

Day of all the week the best, Em-blem of e - ter - nal rest.
Now, from world-ly care set free, May we rest this day in Thee.
Thus may all our Sab - baths prove Fore-tastes of the joys a - bove. A - MEN.

Copyright, 1897, by The Century Co.

10. Now, when the dusky shades of night.

THE LORD'S DAY. MORNING.

B. H. Kennedy, 1863.   J. Stainer, 1872.

1. Now, when the dusk-y shades of night re-treat-ing Be-fore the sun's red ban-ner swift-ly flee; Now, when the ter-rors of the dark are fleet-ing, O Lord, we lift our thank-ful hearts to Thee.

2. Look from the height of heav'n, and send to cheer us Thy light and truth, and guide us on-ward still; Still let Thy mer-cy, as of old, be near us, And lead us safe-ly to Thy ho-ly Hill. A-men.

3 Lo, when that morn of endless light is waking,
   And shades of evil from its splendors flee,
  Safe may we rise, this earth's dark vale forsaking,
   Through all the long, bright day to dwell with Thee.

4 Be this by Thee, O God thrice holy, granted,
   O Father, Son, and Spirit, ever blest;
  Whose glory by the heav'n and earth is chanted,
   Whose name by men and angels is confess'd. Amen.

THE LORD'S DAY. MORNING

Come, my soul, thou must be waking.   11

German, 1699.
J. STAINER, 1872.

1. Come, my soul, thou must be waking; Now is breaking
2. Glad - ly hail the light re - turn - ing; Read - y burn - ing
3. Pray that He may pros - per ev - er Each en - deav - or,

O'er the earth an - oth - er day: Come! to Him, who made this splendor,
Be the in - cense of thy pow'rs; For the night is safe - ly end - ed;
When thine aim is good and true; But that He may ev - er thwart thee,

See thou rend - er All thy fee - ble strength can pay.
God hath tend - ed With His care Thy help - less hours.
And con - vert thee, When thou e - vil wouldst pur - sue. A - MEN.

4 Only God's free gifts abuse not.
    Light refuse not,
  But His Spirit's voice obey;
  Thou with Him shalt dwell, beholding
    Light unfolding
  All things in unclouded day.

5 Glory, honor, exaltation,
    Adoration,
  Be to the Eternal One;
  To the Father, Son, and Spirit,
    Praise and merit,
  While unending ages run! AMEN.

THE LORD'S DAY. MORNING.

12 Every morning mercies new.

H. Bonar, 1868.
W. W. Gilchrist, 1886.

1. Ev-ery morn-ing mer-cies new Fall as fresh as ear-ly dew;
For Thy mer-cies, Lord, are sure, Thy compas-sion doth en-dure.

2. Still the great-ness of Thy love Dai-ly doth our sins re-move;
Ev-ery morn-ing let us pay Trib-ute with the ear-ly day;

Dai-ly, far as east to west, Lifts the bur-den from the breast;
Gives un-bought to those who pray Strength to stand in e-vil day. A-MEN.

3 Let our pray'rs each morn prevail,
That these gifts may never fail;
And, as we confess the sin
And the tempter's pow'r within,
Feed us with the Bread of Life,
Fit us for our daily strife.

4 As the morning light returns,
As the sun with splendor burns,
Teach us still to turn to Thee,
Ever-blessed Trinity,
With our hands our hearts to raise,
In unfailing pray'r and praise. AMEN.

Copyright, 1887, by The Century Co.

THE LORD'S DAY. MORNING.

Day-spring of Eternity!

German.
Allegro.
J. MOSENTHAL, 1886.

1. Day-spring of E-ter-ni-ty, Brightness of the light di-vine,
2. As on drooping herb and flow'r Lies the soft, re-fresh-ing dew,
3. Let Thy fire of love de-stroy All our earth-ly taint and leav'n;

As the day-light fills the sky, Let Thy beams up-on us shine,
Let Thy Spir-it's fresh-'ning power Dry and faint-ing hearts re-new;
Wake our souls to love and joy, Kindling like the east-ern heav'n;

Scat-t'ring with their glo-rious might All our night.
Show'rs of bless-ing o-ver all Soft-ly fall.
Let us tru-ly rise ere yet Life hath set. A-MEN.

4 Day-spring of eternal skies,
  Grant that on Thine Advent-morn,
From the dust our flesh may rise
  To a nobler being born,
Strong in heav'n its course to run
  As the sun.

5 Sorrowing here we seek Thy face;
  Guide us with Thy cheering ray:
Lead us, glorious Sun of grace,
  To the land of endless day,
Where the joy that bids us rise
  Never dies. AMEN.

Copyright, 1887, by The Century Co.

THE LORD'S DAY. EVENING.

Abide with me!

4 I need Thy presence every passing hour;
What but Thy grace can foil the tempter's pow'r?
Who like Thyself my guide and stay can be?
Through cloud and sunshine, O abide with me!

5 Hold Thou Thy cross before my closing eyes;
Shine through the gloom, and point me to the skies.
Heav'n's morning breaks, and earth's vain shadows flee!
In life, in death, O Lord, abide with me! AMEN.

17. Night's shadows falling.

THE LORD'S DAY. EVENING.

A. T. RUSSELL, 1851.　　F. F. FLEMMING, 1810.

1. Night's shad-ows fall-ing Now to rest are call-ing; Rest we, pos-sess-ing Heav'nly peace and bless-ing; This we im-plore Thee, Fall-ing down be-fore Thee, Great King of glo-ry.

2. O Sav-iour, hear us; Son of God, be near us; Thine an-gels send us; Let Thy love at-tend us. He noth-ing fear-eth Whom Thy pres-ence cheer-eth, Light his path clear-eth. A-MEN.

3 Be near, relieving
　All who now are grieving;
　　Thy visitation
　　Be our consolation;
　O hear the sighing
　Of the faint and dying;
　　Lord, hear our crying.

4 O Lord of Glory
　Praise we and adore Thee,—
　　Thee for us given
　　Our true Rest from heaven;
　Rest, peace, and blessing
　We are now possessing,
　　Thy name confessing. AMEN.

THE LORD'S DAY. EVENING.

19 Sun of my soul!

J. KEBLE, 1827.   "HURSLEY."   German, 1792.

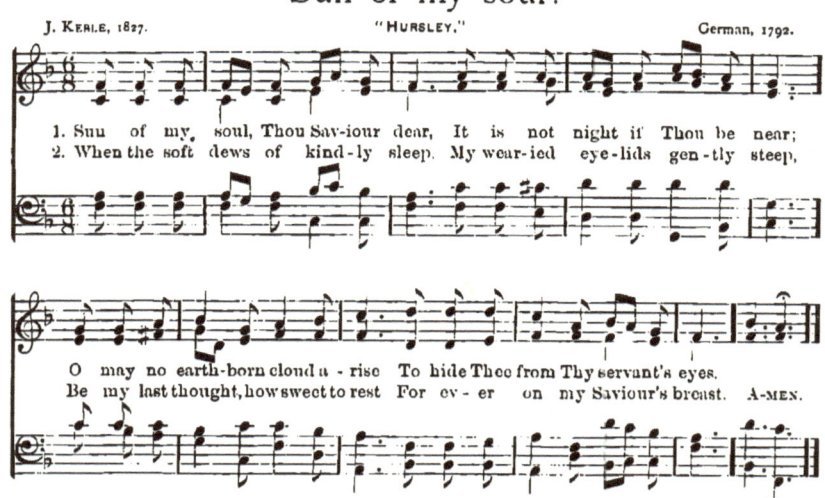

1. Sun of my soul, Thou Saviour dear, It is not night if Thou be near;
O may no earth-born cloud a-rise To hide Thee from Thy servant's eyes.

2. When the soft dews of kindly sleep My wearied eyelids gently steep,
Be my last thought, how sweet to rest For ever on my Saviour's breast. A-MEN.

3 Abide with me from morn till eve,
  For without Thee I cannot live:
  Abide with me when night is nigh,
  For without Thee I dare not die.

4 Come near and bless us when we wake,
  Ere through the world our way we take;
  Till in the ocean of Thy love
  We lose ourselves in heav'n above. AMEN.

20 Saviour, breathe an evening blessing.

J. EDMESTON, 1820.   "NEWTON FERNS."   S. SMITH.
Andante.

1. Saviour, breathe an evening blessing, Ere repose our spirits seal;
2. Tho' the night be dark and dreary, Darkness cannot hide from Thee;
3. Tho' destruction walk around us, Tho' the arrow past us fly,

THE LORD'S DAY. EVENING.   21

The day Thou gavest, Lord, is ended.

J. ELLERTON.   "ST. CLEMENT."   C. C. SCHOLEFIELD.
Cantabile.

1. The day Thou gav-est, Lord, is end-ed, The dark-ness falls at
2. We thank Thee that Thy Church un-sleep-ing, While earth rolls on-ward
3. As o'er each con-ti-nent and is-land The dawn leads on an-

Thy be-hest; To Thee our morn-ing hymns as-cend-ed; Thy praise shall
in - to light, Thro' all the world her watch is keep-ing, And nev-er
oth - er day, The voice of pray'r is nev - er si - lent, Nor dies the

hal - low now our rest.
rests by day or night.
strain of praise a - way.   AMEN.

4 The sun, that bids us rest, is waking
  Our brethren 'neath the western sky,
  And hour by hour fresh lips are making
  Thy wondrous doings heard on high.

5 So be it, Lord; Thy throne shall never,
  Like earth's proud empires, pass away;
  But stand, and rule, and grow for ever,
  Till all Thy creatures own Thy sway. AMEN.

Saviour, breathe an evening blessing.—*Concluded.*

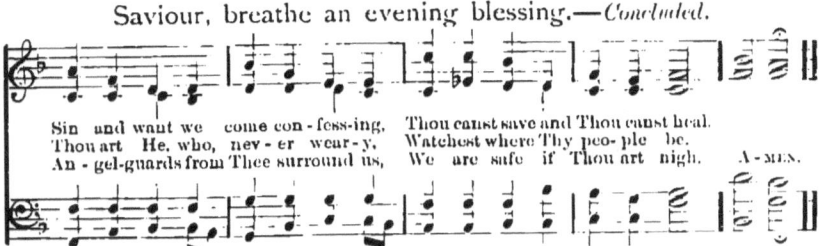

Sin and want we come con - fess-ing,   Thou canst save and Thou canst heal.
Thou art He, who, nev - er wear - y,   Watchest where Thy peo - ple be.
An - gel-guards from Thee surround us, We are safe if Thou art nigh.   A-MEN.

THE LORD'S DAY. EVENING

The shadows of the evening hours. 23

Miss A. A. Proctor. 1858.   "ST. LEONARD."   H. Hiles.

Cantabile.

1. The shad-ows of the eve-ning hours Fall from the dark-'ning sky,
2. The sor-rows of Thy ser-vants, Lord, O do not Thou de-spise,
3. Slow-ly the rays of day-light fade; So fade with-in the heart

Up - on the fragrance of the flow'rs The dews of eve-ning lie;
But let the in-cense of our pray'rs Be-fore Thy mer-cy rise;
The hopes of earth-ly love and joy, That one by one de-part;

Be - fore Thy throne, O Lord of heav'n, We kneel at close of day;
The brightness of the com-ing night Up - on the dark-ness rolls;
Slow - ly the bright stars, one by one, With - in the heav-ens shine:—

Look on Thy child-ren from on high, And hear us while we pray.
With hopes of fu - ture glo - ry chase The shadows from our souls.
Give us, O Lord, fresh hopes in heav'n, And trust in things di - vine. A-MEN.

THE LORD'S DAY. EVENING.

24 God the Father, be Thou near.

G. RAWSON, 1858. R. REDHEAD, 1852.
Quietly.

1. God the Fa-ther, be Thou near, Save from ev-ery harm to-night;
2. God the Sav-iour, be our Peace, Put a-way our sins to-night;

Make us all Thy chil-dren dear, In the dark-ness be our Light.
Speak the word of full re-lease, Turn our darkness in-to light. A-MEN.

3 Holy Spirit, deign to come,
  Sanctify us all to-night;
  In our hearts prepare Thy home,
  Turn our darkness into light.

4 Holy Trinity, be nigh,
  Mystery of love ador'd;
  Help to live and help to die;
  Lighten all our darkness, Lord. AMEN.

25 Again, as evening's shadow falls.

S. LONGFELLOW, 1859. "TERRY." R. DE W. MALLARY, 1885.
Andante.

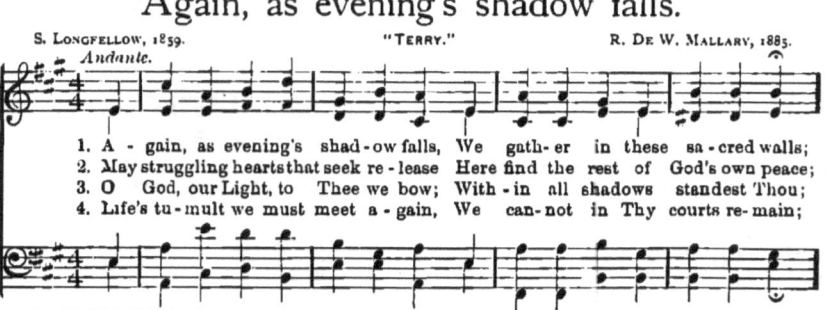

1. A-gain, as evening's shad-ow falls, We gath-er in these sa-cred walls;
2. May struggling hearts that seek re-lease Here find the rest of God's own peace;
3. O God, our Light, to Thee we bow; With-in all shadows standest Thou;
4. Life's tu-mult we must meet a-gain, We can-not in Thy courts re-main;

Copyright, 1887, by The Century Co.

THE LORD'S DAY. EVENING.

The radiant morn hath passed away.

G. THRING, 1864.   "WOODTHORPE."   J. ADCOCK

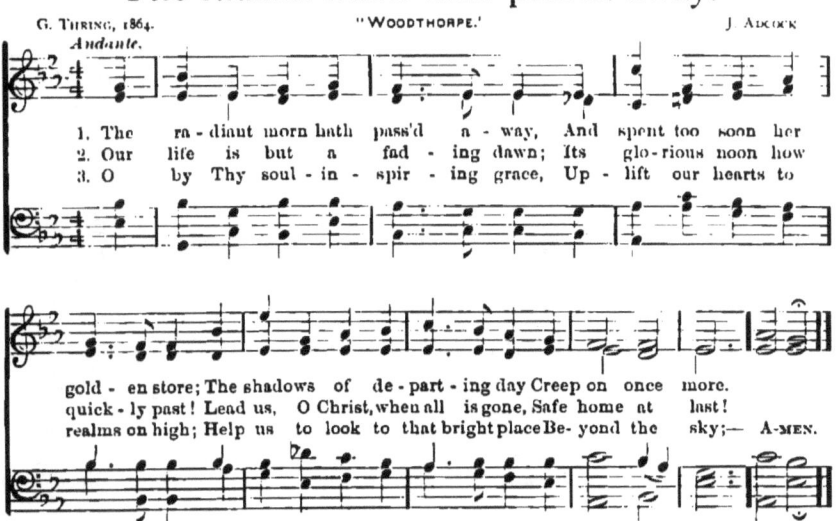

1. The ra-diant morn hath pass'd a-way, And spent too soon her gold-en store; The shadows of de-part-ing day Creep on once more.
2. Our life is but a fad-ing dawn; Its glo-rious noon how quick-ly past! Lead us, O Christ, when all is gone, Safe home at last!
3. O by Thy soul-in-spir-ing grace, Up-lift our hearts to realms on high; Help us to look to that bright place Be-yond the sky;— A-MEN.

4 Where light and life and joy and peace
In undivided empire reign,
And thronging angels never cease
Their deathless strain;—

5 Where saints are cloth'd in spotless white,
And evening shadows never fall;
Where Thou, eternal Light of light,
Art Lord of all! AMEN.

Again, as evening's shadow falls.—*Concluded.*

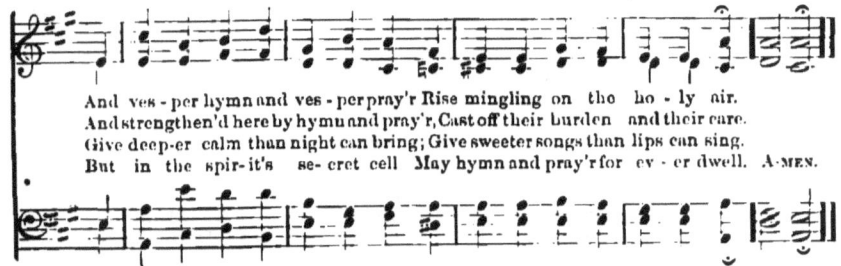

And ves-per hymn and ves-per pray'r Rise mingling on the ho-ly air.
And strengthen'd here by hymn and pray'r, Cast off their burden and their care.
Give deep-er calm than night can bring; Give sweeter songs than lips can sing.
But in the spir-it's se-cret cell May hymn and pray'r for ev-er dwell. A-MEN.

27. Sweet Saviour, bless us ere we go.

THE LORD'S DAY. EVENING.

F. W. FABER, 1849.   "VALETE."   A. S. SULLIVAN, 1874.

Andante.

1. Sweet Saviour, bless us ere we go, Thy word in-to our minds in-stil,
   And make our lukewarm hearts to glow With low-ly love and fer-vent will.
2. The day is done, its hours have run; And Thou hast tak-en count of all—
   The scan-ty triumphs grace hath won, The brok-en vow, the fre-quent fall.
3. Do more than par-don; give us joy, Sweet fear, and so-ber lib-er-ty,
   And sim-ple hearts with-out al-loy, That on-ly long to be like Thee.
4. All toil is blest, for Thou hast toil'd, And care is light, for Thou hast car'd:
   Let not our works by strife be soil'd, Or by de-ceit our hearts ensnar'd.

REFRAIN.

Thro' life's long day, and death's dark night, O gen-tle Je-sus, be our Light. A-MEN.

    5 For all we love, the poor, the sad,
      The sinful, unto Thee we call;
      O let Thy mercy make us glad:
      Thou art our Saviour, and our All.—REF.

    6 Sweet Saviour, bless us! night is come;
      Through night and darkness near us be;
      Good angels watch about our home,
      And we are one day nearer Thee!—REF. AMEN.

THE LORD'S DAY. EVENING.

Glory to Thee, my God, this night.

THOMAS KEN, 1697. J. R. FAIRLAMB, 1886.

1. Glo-ry to Thee, my God, this night, For all the bless-ings
2. For-give me, Lord, for Thy dear Son, The ill which I this
3. Teach me to live, that I may dread The grave as lit-tle

of the light; Keep me, O keep me, King of kings!
day have done; That with the world, my-self, and Thee,
as my bed: Teach me to die, that so I may

Be-neath Thine own al-might-y wings.
I, ere I sleep, at peace may be.
Rise glo-rious at the judg-ment-day. A - - - MEN.

4 O let my soul on Thee repose,
  And may sweet sleep mine eyelids close!
  Sleep, which shall me more vigorous make,
  To serve my God when I awake.

5 Praise God, from Whom all blessings flow;
  Praise Him, all creatures here below;
  Praise Him above, ye heav'nly host;
  Praise Father, Son, and Holy Ghost! AMEN.

Copyright, 1897, by The Century Co.

Songs of the Lord's House.

Father, again in Jesus' name we meet. 30

1. Father, again in Je-sus' name we meet, And bow in pen-i-tence be-neath Thy feet: A-gain to Thee our fee-ble voi-ces raise, To sue for mer-cy, and to sing Thy praise.
2. O we would bless Thee for Thy cease-less care, And all Thy work from day to day de-clare! Is not our life with hour-ly mer-cies crown'd? Does not Thine arm en-cir-cle us a-round?
3. We are un-worth-y of Thy bound-less love, Too oft with care-less feet from Thee we rove; But now, en-cour-aged by Thy voice, we come, Re-turn-ing sin-ners, to a Fa-ther's home.
4. O by that name in which all ful-ness dwells, O by that love which ev-ery love ex-cels, O by that blood so free-ly shed for sin, O-pen blest mer-cy's gate, and take us in! A-MEN.

THE LORD'S HOUSE. OPENING OF SERVICE.

Pleasant are Thy courts.

H. F. Lyte, 1834.
W. B. Gilbert, 1862.

1. Pleas-ant are Thy courts a-bove In the land of light and love;
   Pleas-ant are Thy courts be-low In this land of sin and woe.
2. Hap-py birds that sing and fly Round Thy al-tars, O Most High!
   Hap-pier souls that find a rest In a heav'n-ly Fa-ther's breast!

Oh, my spir-it longs and faints For the con-verse of Thy saints,
Like the wand-'ring dove, that found No re-pose on earth a-round,

For the brightness of Thy face, For Thy ful-ness, God of grace!
They can to their ark re-pair And en-joy it ev-er there. A-MEN.

By permission.

3 Happy souls! Their praises flow
  Even in this vale of woe;
  Waters in the desert rise,
  Manna feeds them from the skies:
  On they go from strength to strength
  Till they reach Thy throne at length,
  At Thy feet adoring fall,
  Who hast led them safe through all.

4 Lord! be mine this prize to win;
  Guide me through a world of sin;
  Keep me by Thy saving grace;
  Give me at Thy side a place.
  Sun and shield alike Thou art:
  Guide and guard my erring heart.
  Grace and glory flow from Thee;
  Shower, O shower them, Lord, on me! AMEN.

33. Sweet is the work, O Lord.

THE LORD'S HOUSE. OPENING OF SERVICE.

Miss H. Auber, 1829.
E. G. Monk, 1867.
Con moto.

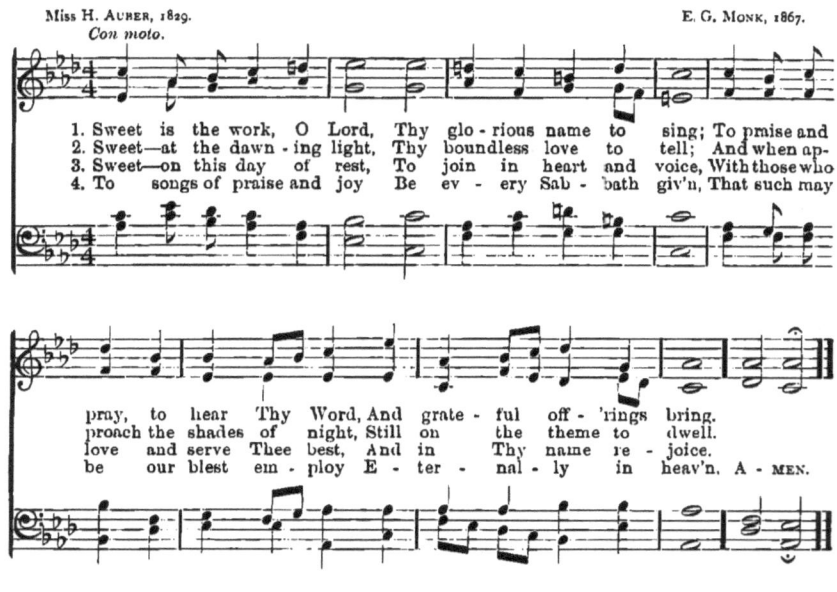

1. Sweet is the work, O Lord, Thy glorious name to sing; To praise and pray, to hear Thy Word, And grateful off-'rings bring.
2. Sweet—at the dawning light, Thy boundless love to tell; And when approach the shades of night, Still on the theme to dwell.
3. Sweet—on this day of rest, To join in heart and voice, With those who love and serve Thee best, And in Thy name rejoice.
4. To songs of praise and joy Be every Sabbath giv'n, That such may be our blest employ Eternally in heav'n. A-MEN.

34. How amiable are Thy tabernacles!

From Psalm 84.
G. F. Händel.

1 How amiable are Thy tabernacles, O | Lord of | Hosts! ‖
  My soul longeth, yea, even fainteth | for the | courts • of the | Lord.

3 They go from | strength to | strength, ‖
  Every one of them appeareth be- | fore | God in | Zion.

5 Glory to the Father, | and • to the | Son, ‖
  And | to the | Holy | Ghost;

THE LORD'S HOUSE. OPENING OF SERVICE.

Stand up and bless the Lord.

J. MONTGOMERY, 1825.   "BEN RHYDDING."   A. R. REINAGLE.

1. Stand up and bless the Lord, Ye peo-ple of His choice; Stand up, and bless the Lord your God, With heart and soul and voice.
2. Tho' high a-bove all praise, A-bove all bless-ing high, Who would not fear His ho-ly name And laud, and mag-ni-fy?
3. O for the liv-ing flame, From His own al-tar brought, To touch our lips, our minds in-spire, And wing to heav'n our thought. A-MEN.

4 God is our strength and song,
　And His salvation ours;
Then be His love in Christ proclaim'd,
　With all our ransom'd pow'rs.

5 Stand up, and bless the Lord;
　The Lord your God adore:
Stand up, and bless His glorious name,
　Henceforth for evermore. AMEN.

How amiable are Thy tabernacles!—*Concluded.*

2 Blessed are they that | dwell · in Thy | House; |
　They will be | still praising | Thee.
4 For a day in Thy courts is better | than a | thousand; |
　I had rather stand at the threshold of the House of my God
　than to | dwell · in the | tents of · wickedness.
6 As it was in the beginning, is now, and | ever shall be, ||
　World without | end: A- | men.

THE LORD'S HOUSE. OPENING OF SERVICE.

Come forth, O Christian brothers!

J. ELLERTON.
Con brio.
"LANCASHIRE."
H. SMART, 1836. (?)

1. Come forth, O Christian broth-ers, In or-der'd, fair ar-ray;
2. Le-vites of that new tem-ple Not built by hu-man hands,
3. Be-fore Thy throne great an-gels With veil-ed fa-ces bow;
4. So, kin-dled from Thine al-tar, Pre-par'd and own'd by Thee;

Come forth, with strains of glad-ness, To greet your fes-tal Day!
Be-fore whose heav'nly al-tar Our Priest for ev-er stands;
Have mer-cy on the sin-ful Who dare to seek Thee now;
Shall bod-y, soul, and spir-it, A whole, rich off-'ring be;

Re-joice in God your Sav-iour; Your hearts and voi-ces raise,
Thro' Him our gifts we of-fer, Thro' Him our vows we pay,
And o'er our earth-soil'd gar-ments Thy robe of whiteness fling,
So with th'e-ter-nal an-them Our prais-es shall u-nite,

His gates with songs to en-ter; And tread His courts with praise!
The fruit of hearts made read-y To give Him thanks to-day.
And touch with fire su-per-nal Our lips be-fore we sing!
And this, our low-ly ser-vice, Be pleas-ing in Thy sight. A-MEN.

THE LORD'S HOUSE. OPENING OF SERVICE.   37

Come, Thou almighty King!

C. WESLEY, 1757.   "ITALIAN HYMN."   F. GIARDINI, 1769.

1. Come, Thou almighty King, Help us Thy name to sing, Help us to praise: Father all-glorious, O'er all victorious, Come, and reign over us, Ancient of Days!

2. Come, Thou incarnate Word, Gird on Thy mighty sword: Our pray'r attend; Come, and Thy people bless, And give Thy Word success, Spirit of holiness, On us descend! A-MEN.

3 Come, holy Comforter,
   Thy sacred witness bear,
   In this glad hour:
   Thou, who almighty art,
   Now rule in every heart,
   And ne'er from us depart,
   Spirit of pow'r!

4 To the great One in Three,
   The highest praises be,
   Hence evermore!
   His sov'reign majesty
   May we in glory see,
   And to eternity
   Love and adore. AMEN.

38   With joy we lift our eyes.

THE LORD'S HOUSE. OPENING OF SERVICE.

T. Jervis, 1795.   "PACKINGTON."   J. Black.
With energy.

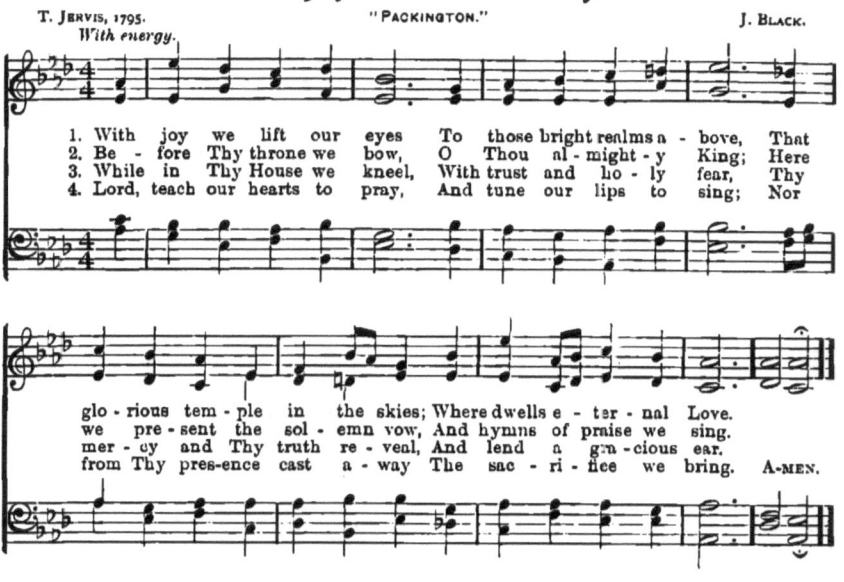

1. With joy we lift our eyes To those bright realms a-bove, That glo-rious tem-ple in the skies; Where dwells e-ter-nal Love.
2. Be-fore Thy throne we bow, O Thou al-might-y King; Here we pre-sent the sol-emn vow, And hymns of praise we sing.
3. While in Thy House we kneel, With trust and ho-ly fear, Thy mer-cy and Thy truth re-veal, And lend a gra-cious ear.
4. Lord, teach our hearts to pray, And tune our lips to sing; Nor from Thy pres-ence cast a-way The sac-ri-fice we bring. A-MEN.

39   Make a joyful noise unto the Lord.

Psalm 100.   "JUBILATE DEO."   W. Crotch.

1 Make a joyful noise unto the Lord, | all ye | lands; ||
   Serve the Lord with gladness, come be- | fore His | presence with | singing.

3 Enter into His gates with thanksgiving, and into His | courts with | praise; ||
   Give thanks unto | Him, and | bless His | name;

5 Glory be to the Father, | and · to the | Son,
   And | to the | Holy Ghost;

THE LORD'S HOUSE. OPENING OF SERVICE.　　　　　　　　40

My God, is any hour so sweet?

Miss C. Elliott, 1834.　　　　　　　　　　　　　　　　J. Naylor.

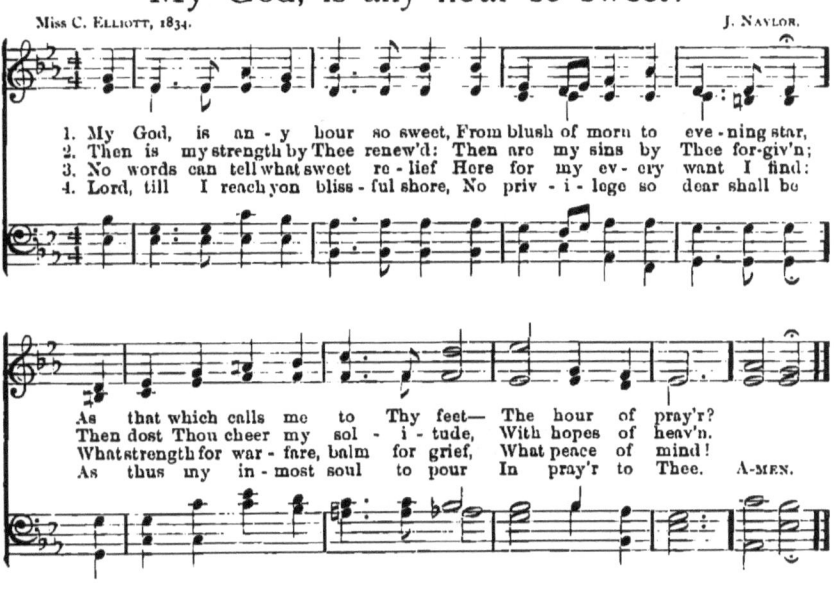

1. My God, is an-y hour so sweet, From blush of morn to eve-ning star,
2. Then is my strength by Thee renew'd: Then are my sins by Thee for-giv'n;
3. No words can tell what sweet re-lief Here for my ev-ery want I find:
4. Lord, till I reach yon bliss-ful shore, No priv-i-lege so dear shall be

As that which calls me to Thy feet— The hour of pray'r?
Then dost Thou cheer my sol - i - tude, With hopes of heav'n.
What strength for war-fare, balm for grief, What peace of mind!
As thus my in-most soul to pour In pray'r to Thee. A-MEN.

Make a joyful noise unto the Lord!—*Concluded.*

2 Know ye that the Lord, He is God; it is He that hath made us, and | we are | His. ‖
　We are His people, and the | sheep of | His | pasture.
4 For the Lord is good: His mercy en- | dureth for | ever, ‖
　And His faithfulness | unto | all gener- | ations.
6 As it was in the beginning, is now, and | ever | shall be, ‖
　World | without | end: A- | MEN.

41. Angel-voices ever singing.

F. Pott, 1861.   "Angel-Voices."   *A. S. Sullivan, 1872.*

1. An-gel voic-es, ev-er sing-ing Round Thy throne of light—
2. Thou, who art be-yond the far-thest Mor-tal eye can scan,
3. Yes, we know Thy love re-joi-ces O'er each work of Thine;

An-gel harps, for ev-er ring-ing, Rest not day nor night; Thousands
Can it be that Thou re-gard-est Songs of sin-ful man? Can we
Thou didst ears and hands and voic-es For Thy praise com-bine; Po-et's

on-ly live to bless Thee, And con-fess Thee, Lord of might
feel that Thou art near us, And wilt hear us? Yes, we can.
art and mu-sic's measure For Thy pleas-ure Didst de-sign. A-men.

4 In Thy house, great God, we offer
  Of Thine own to Thee;
And for Thine acceptance proffer,
  All unworthily,
Hearts and minds, and hands and voices,
In our choicest
  Melody.

5 Honor, glory, might, and merit,
  Thine shall ever be,
Father, Son, and Holy Spirit,
  Blessed Trinity!
Of the best that Thou hast given,
Earth and heaven
  Render Thee! Amen.

45. Lord, Thy Word abideth.

THE LORD'S HOUSE. THE WORD.

H. W. Baker, 1861.   "St. Cyprian."   R. R. Chope, 1862.

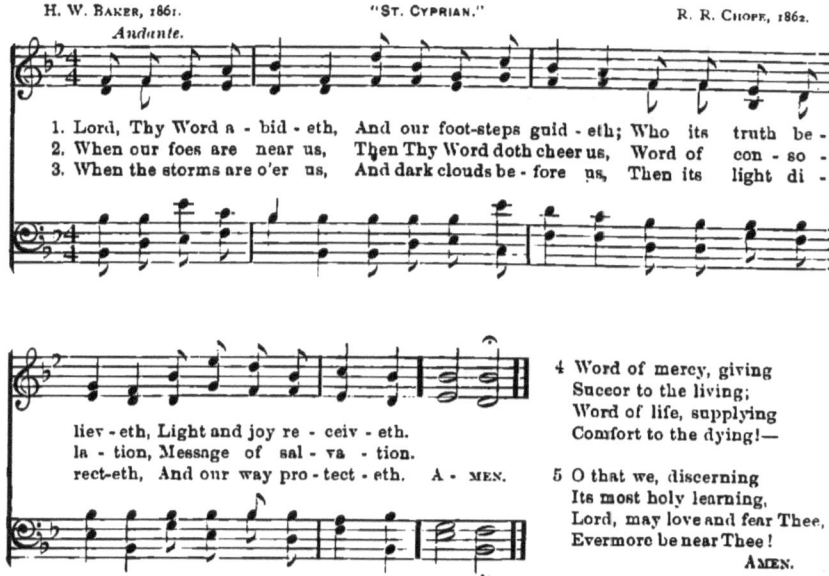

1. Lord, Thy Word a-bid-eth, And our foot-steps guid-eth; Who its truth be-liev-eth, Light and joy re-ceiv-eth.
2. When our foes are near us, Then Thy Word doth cheer us, Word of con-so-la-tion, Message of sal-va-tion.
3. When the storms are o'er us, And dark clouds be-fore us, Then its light di-rect-eth, And our way pro-tect-eth. A-MEN.

4 Word of mercy, giving
Succor to the living;
Word of life, supplying
Comfort to the dying!—

5 O that we, discerning
Its most holy learning,
Lord, may love and fear Thee,
Evermore be near Thee!
AMEN.

46. Father of mercies, in Thy Word.

Miss A. Steele, 1760.   G. M. Garrett, 1872.

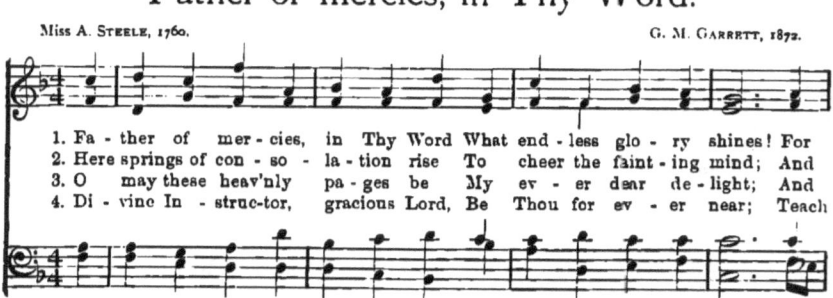

1. Fa-ther of mer-cies, in Thy Word What end-less glo-ry shines! For
2. Here springs of con-so-la-tion rise To cheer the faint-ing mind; And
3. O may these heav'nly pa-ges be My ev-er dear de-light; And
4. Di-vine In-struc-tor, gracious Lord, Be Thou for ev-er near; Teach

THE LORD'S HOUSE. THE WORD.

Almighty God, Thy Word is cast. 47

J. Cawood, 1815?   "CHILDHOOD."   C. J. Dickinson, 1861.
Andante.

1. Al - might - y God, Thy Word is cast Like seed up - on the ground;
2. Let not the foe of Christ and man This ho - ly seed re - move;
3. Let not the world's de-ceit - ful cares The ris - ing plant de - stroy;
4. Great God, come down, and on Thy Word Thy might - y pow'r be - stow,

O may it grow in hum-ble hearts, And righteous fruits a - bound.
But give it root in pray-ing souls To bring forth fruits of love.
But let it yield an hundred - fold The fruits of peace and joy.
That all who hear the joy - ful sound, Thy sav - ing grace may know. A - MEN.

Father of mercies, in Thy Word.—*Concluded.*

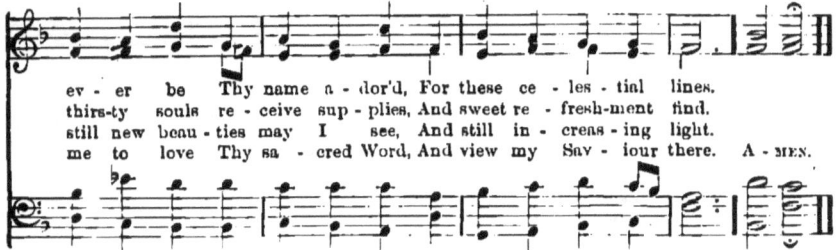

ev - er be Thy name a - dor'd, For these ce - les - tial lines.
thirs-ty souls re - ceive sup - plies, And sweet re - fresh-ment find.
still new beau - ties may I see, And still in - creas - ing light.
me to love Thy sa - cred Word, And view my Sav - iour there. A - MEN.

THE LORD'S HOUSE. THE WORD.

48 Lamp of our feet, whereby we trace.

B. BARTON.   "JAZER."   A. E. TOZER.

1. Lamp of our feet, where-by we trace Our path when wont to stray; Stream from the fount of heav'n-ly grace; Brook by the trav-'ler's way;
2. Bread of our souls, where-on we feed; True man-na from on high; Our guide and chart, where-in we read Of realms be-yond the sky;
3. Pil-lar of fire, through watches dark, Or ra-diant cloud by day; When waves would whelm our toss-ing bark, Our anch-or and our stay;
4. Word of the ev-er-liv-ing God; Will of His glo-rious Son; With-out thee how could earth be trod, Or heav'n it-self be won! A-MEN.

5 Yet, to unfold thy hidden worth,
   Thy mysteries to reveal,
That Spirit which first gave thee forth
   Thy volume must unseal.

6 And we, if we aright would learn
   The wisdom it imparts,
Must to its heav'nly teaching turn
   With simple, childlike hearts. AMEN.

49 Thy Word is a lamp unto my feet.

From Psalm 119.   J. ROBINSON.

1 Thy Word is a lamp unto my feet, and light | unto my | path; ||
   Thy testimonies have I taken as a | heri- | tage for | ever.

3 The opening of Thy | words giveth | light; ||
   It giveth under- | standing | to the | simple.

5 Glory be to the Father, | and • to the | Son, ||
   And | to the | Holy | Ghost;

THE LORD'S HOUSE. THE WORD.

Thy Word is like a garden, Lord.

E. HODDER, 1868.   "ST. DIONIS."   J. GOODWIN.

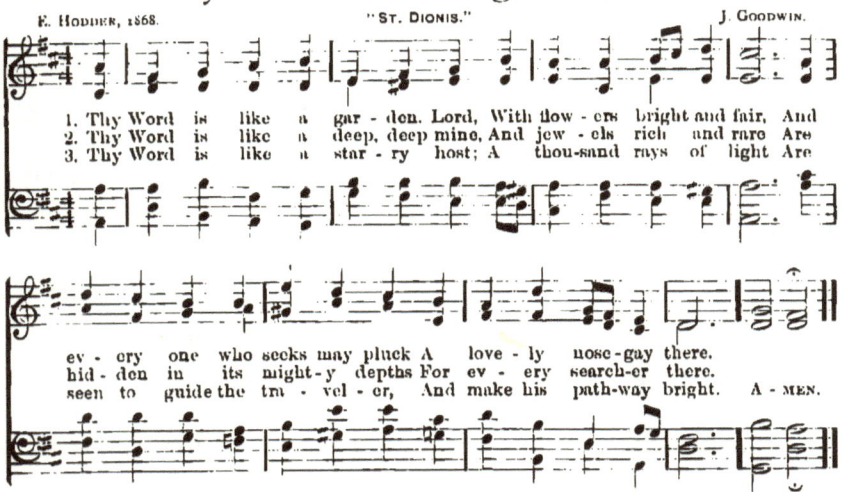

1. Thy Word is like a gar-den, Lord, With flow-ers bright and fair, And
2. Thy Word is like a deep, deep mine, And jew-els rich and rare Are
3. Thy Word is like a star-ry host; A thou-sand rays of light Are

ev-ery one who seeks may pluck A love-ly nose-gay there.
hid-den in its might-y depths For ev-ery search-er there.
seen to guide the tra-vel-er, And make his path-way bright. A-MEN.

4 Thy Word is like a glorious choir,
  And loud its anthems ring;
  Though many tongues and parts unite,
  It is one song they sing.
5 Thy Word is like an armory,
  Where soldiers may repair,
  And find for life's long battle-day
  All needful weapons there.

6 O may I love Thy precious Word;
  May I explore the mine;
  May I its fragrant flowers glean;
  May light upon me shine.
7 O may I find my armor there,
  Thy Word my trusty sword;
  I'll learn to fight with every foe
  The battle of the Lord.   AMEN.

Thy Word is a lamp unto my feet.—*Concluded.*

2 Thou art my hiding-place and my shield: I | hope · in Thy | Word; ||
  I love Thy commandments above gold, | yea, a- | bove fine | gold.
4 Let my lips utter praise, for Thou teachest | me Thy | statutes; ||
  Let my tongue sing of Thy Word, for all Thy com- | mandments are | righteous- | ness.
6 As it was in the beginning, is now, and ever | shall be, |
  World | without | end: A- | MEN.

51. Saviour, again to Thy dear name.

THE LORD'S HOUSE. CLOSE OF SERVICE.

J. ELLERTON, 1866. J. BARNBY, 1872.

1. Sav-iour, a-gain to Thy dear name we raise With one ac-cord our part-ing hymn of praise; We stand to bless Thee ere our wor-ship cease; Then low-ly kneel-ing, wait Thy word of peace.

2. Grant us Thy peace up-on our home-ward way; With Thee be-gan, with Thee shall end the day; Guard Thou the lips from sin, the hearts from shame, That in this house have call'd up-on Thy name. A-MEN.

3 Grant us Thy peace, Lord, through the coming night;
Turn Thou for us its darkness into light;
From harm and danger keep Thy children free,
For dark and light are both alike to Thee.

4 Grant us Thy peace throughout our earthly life,
Our balm in sorrow, and our stay in strife;
Then, when Thy voice shall bid our conflict cease,
Call us, O Lord, to Thine eternal peace. AMEN.

Holy Offerings.—*Concluded.*

laid	we	leave	them; Christ, pre-sent them!	God,	re-ceive them!
to	out-live	them; Christ, a-tone for!	God,	for-give them!
we	de-plore	them, Je-sus, plead for!	God,	re-store them! A-MEN.

4 Homage of each humble heart
Ere we from Thy house depart;
Worship fervent, deep and high.
Adoration, ecstacy;
All that childlike love can render
Of devotion true and tender—
On Thine altar laid we leave them:
Christ, present them! God, receive them!

5 To the Father, and the Son,
And the Spirit, Three in One,
Though our mortal weakness mise
Off'rings of imperfect praise,
Yet with hearts bow'd down most lowly,
Crying Holy! Holy! Holy!
On Thine altar laid we leave them;
Christ, present them! God, receive them!
AMEN.

Now to Him who loved us. 55

S. M. WARING, 1826.　　　"MURIEL."　　　C. GOUNOD.

Now to Him that lov'd us, gave us Ev-ery pledge that love can give.

Free-ly shed His blood to save us, Gave His life that we might live,

Be the king-dom and do-min-ion And the glo-ry ev-er-more. A-MEN.

56 Of Thy love some gracious token.

THE LORD'S HOUSE. CLOSE OF SERVICE.

T. KELLY, 1802.   "ST. LUCIAN."   A. S. SULLIVAN, 1868.

Of Thy love some gra-cious to-ken Grant us, Lord, be-fore we go; Bless Thy word which has been spok-en; Life and peace on all be-stow. When we join the world a-gain, Let our hearts with Thee re-main; O di-rect us, And pro-tect us, Till we gain the heav'n-ly shore, Where Thy peo-ple want no more. A-MEN.

Songs of Adoration.

Holy! Holy! Holy!

Holy, Holy, Holy!

ADORATION

58

R. Heber, 1827.   "NICAEA."   J. B. Dykes, 1860.

1. Ho-ly, Ho-ly, Ho-ly! Lord God Al-might-y! Ear-ly in the morn-ing our song shall rise to Thee; Ho-ly, Ho-ly, Ho-ly! Mer-ci-ful and Might-y! God in three per-sons, blessed Trin-i-ty!
2. Ho-ly, Ho-ly, Ho-ly! All the saints a-dore Thee, Casting down their golden crowns around the glass-y sea; Cher-u-bim and sera-phim fall-ing down be-fore Thee, Which wert, and art, and ev-er-more shalt be! A-MEN.

3 Holy, Holy, Holy! Though the darkness hide Thee,
Though the eye of sinful man Thy glory may not see;
Only Thou art holy, there is none beside Thee
Perfect in power, in love, and purity.

4 Holy, Holy, Holy! Lord God Almighty!
All Thy works shall praise Thy name in earth and sky and sea.
Holy, Holy, Holy! Merciful and Mighty!
God in three persons, blessed Trinity! AMEN.

ADORATION.

60 We praise Thee, O God!
"TE DEUM."

Latin, 3d or 4th Century.   PART I.   W. RUSSELL.

1 We praise Thee, O God; we acknowledge Thee to | be the | Lord.‖
  All the earth doth worship Thee, the | Father | ever- | lasting.
3 "Holy, holy, holy, Lord | God of | Sabaoth;‖
  Heav'n and earth are full of the | majes-ty | of Thy | glory."
5 The noble army of | martyrs | praise Thee;‖
  The holy Church throughout all the | world • doth ac- | knowledge|Thee,

PART II.   J. GOSS.

7 Thou art the King of Glory, O Christ!
  Thou art the everlasting | Son • of the | Father.‖
  When Thou tookest upon Thee to deliver man,
  Thou didst humble Thy- | self • to be | born • of a | virgin.
9 Thou sittest at the right hand of God,
  In the glory | of the | Father:‖
  We believe that Thou shalt | come to | be our | Judge:

PART III.   P. HENLEY.

11 O Lord, save Thy people, and | bless Thy | heritage;‖
   Govern them and | lift them | up for | ever.
13 Vouchsafe, O Lord, to keep us this | day without | sin:‖
   O Lord, have mercy upon us, have | mer- | cy up- | on us;

ADORATION.

We praise Thee, O God!—*Concluded.*

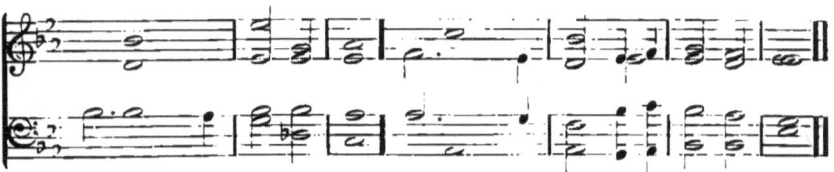

2 To Thee all angels cry aloud; the heav'ns and all the pow'rs there- in. |
To Thee cherubim and seraphim con- | tinual- | ly do | cry,—

4 The glorious company of the a- | postles | praise Thee. ||
The goodly fellowship of the | prophets | praise | Thee.

6 The Father, of an infinite majesty; Thine adorable, true and | only | Son. ||
Also the Holy | Ghost, the | Comfort- | er.

8 When thou hadst overcome the | sharpness of | death, ||
Thou didst open the kingdom of | Heav'n to | all be- | lievers.

10 We therefore pray Thee, help Thy servants,
Whom Thou hast redeem'd with Thy | precious | blood; ||
Make them to be number'd with Thy saints
In | glory | ever- | lasting.

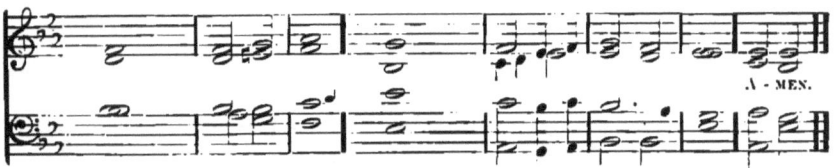

A - MEN.

12 Day by day we magni-fy | Thee; ||
And we worship Thy name, | ever, | world with-out | end.

14 O Lord, let Thy mercy be upon us, as our | trust • is in | Thee; ||
O Lord, in Thee have I trusted;
Let me never | be con- | founded. ||A-MEN.||

61. Lord of all being, throned afar.

ADORATION.

O. W. Holmes, 1848. "ALSTONE." C. E. Willing.

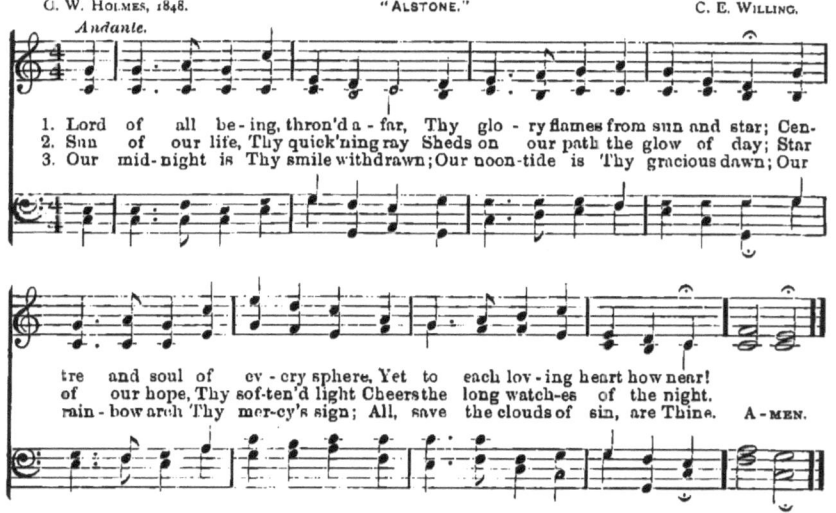

1. Lord of all be-ing, thron'd a-far, Thy glo-ry flames from sun and star; Cen-tre and soul of ev-ery sphere, Yet to each lov-ing heart how near!
2. Sun of our life, Thy quick'ning ray Sheds on our path the glow of day; Star of our hope, Thy sof-ten'd light Cheers the long watch-es of the night.
3. Our mid-night is Thy smile withdrawn; Our noon-tide is Thy gracious dawn; Our rain-bow arch Thy mer-cy's sign; All, save the clouds of sin, are Thine. A-MEN.

4 Lord of all life, below, above,
Whose light is truth, whose warmth is love,
Before Thy ever-blazing throne
We ask no lustre of our own.

5 Grant us Thy truth to make us free,
And kindling hearts that burn for Thee,
Till all Thy living altars claim
One holy light, one heav'nly flame! AMEN.

62. My God, how wonderful Thou art!

F. W. Faber, 1849. "LAMBETH." English.

1. My God, how won-der-ful Thou art! Thy maj-es-ty how bright!
2. How won-der-ful, how beau-ti-ful, The sight of Thee must be,—
3. Yet I may love Thee too, O Lord, Al-might-y as Thou art;
4. No earth-ly fa-ther loves like Thee, No moth-er e'er so mild,

From "Hutchins' S. S. Hymnal," by permission

ADORATION.

O God, our Help in ages past.

63

I. WATTS, 1719.   "ST. ANN'S."   W. CROFT, 1708.

1. O God, our Help in a - ges past, Our Hope for years to come,
2. Be - fore the hills in or - der stood, Or earth re - ceiv'd her frame,
3. A thou-sand a - ges in Thy sight Are like an eve - ning gone;

Our Shel - ter from the storm - y blast, And our e - ter - nal Home!
From ev - er - last - ing Thou art God, To end - less years the same.
Short as the watch that ends the night, Be - fore the ris - ing sun. A-MEN.

4 Time, like an ever-rolling stream,
   Bears all its sons away;
They fly, forgotten, as a dream
   Dies at the opening day.

5 O God, our Help in ages past,
   Our Hope for years to come;
Be Thou our Guard while troubles last,
   And our eternal Home! AMEN.

My God, how wonderful Thou art!—*Concluded.*

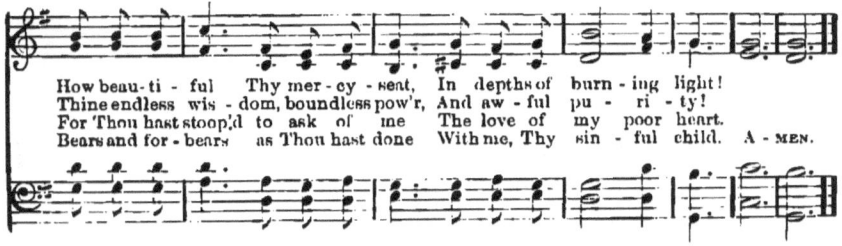

How beau - ti - ful Thy mer - cy - seat, In depths of burn - ing light!
Thine endless wis - dom, boundless pow'r, And aw - ful pu - ri - ty!
For Thou hast stoop'd to ask of me The love of my poor heart.
Bears and for - bears as Thou hast done With me, Thy sin - ful child. A - MEN.

ADORATION

Hark! hark! the organ loudly peals.—*Concluded.*

Ye heav'ns and earth re-joice! And ev-ery heart and voice Your joyous strains up-
Who left His throne on high, And low-ly came to die, That we from earth might

raise   In notes of endless praise   Before His Throne for ev - er, for ev - er!
rise   To realms beyond the skies,   And live with Him for ev - er, for ev - er!

3 Hark! hark! the organ loudly peals,
  Our thankful hearts inviting
To sing the Holy Spirit's praise,
  Both rich and poor uniting;
    Who bids us flee from sin,
    And makes us pure within,
  Till, warm'd with heav'nly love,
  We yearn to sing above
Glad songs of praise for ever!

4 Hark! hark! the organ loudly peals,
  Our thankful hearts inviting
To high upraise our songs of praise,
  Both rich and poor uniting!
    To God the Father, Son,
    And Spirit, Three in One,
  Till, soaring higher and higher,
  We join the heav'nly choir
Before His Throne for ever!   AMEN.

ADORATION

We praise, we bless Thee.—*Concluded.*

70 O worship the King.

ADORATION.

R. GRANT, 1839. "HANOVER." W. CROFT (?), 1708.

1. O worship the King all glorious above, O gratefully sing His pow'r and His love, Our Shield and Defender, the Ancient of days, Pavilion'd in splendor, and girded with praise!

2. O tell of His might, O sing of His grace, Whose robe is the light, whose canopy space. His chariots of wrath the deep thunder-clouds form, And dark is His path on the wings of the storm. A-MEN.

3 Thy bountiful care what tongue can recite?
It breathes in the air, it shines in the light,
It streams from the hills, it descends to the plain,
And sweetly distils in the dew and the rain.

4 Frail children of dust, and feeble as frail,
In Thee do we trust, nor find Thee to fail;
Thy mercies how tender, how firm to the end,
Our Maker, Defender, Redeemer, and Friend! AMEN.

ADORATION OF CHRIST

Ye servants of God.

71

C. WESLEY, 1744. "LYONS." F. J. HAYDN, 1770.

1. Ye ser-vants of God, your Mas-ter pro-claim, And pub-lish a-broad His won-der-ful name; The name all-vic-to-rious of Je-sus ex-tol; His kingdom is glo-rious, He rules o-ver all.
2. God rul-eth on high, al-might-y to save; And still He is nigh, His presence we have; The great con-gre-ga-tion His tri-umph shall sing, As-crib-ing sal-va-tion to Je-sus our King. A-MEN.

3 Salvation to God who sits on the throne,
Let all cry aloud and honor the Son.
The praises of Jesus all angels proclaim,
Fall down on their faces and worship the Lamb.

4 Then let us adore and give Him His right,
All glory and power, all wisdom and might,
All honor and blessing, with angels above;
And thanks never ceasing, and infinite love. AMEN.

ADORATION OF CHRIST.

72 Christ, above all glory seated.

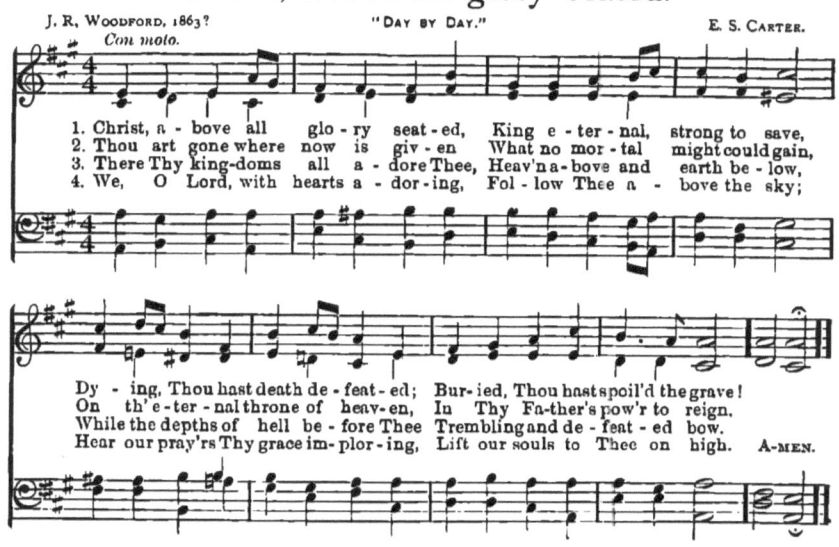

1. Christ, a-bove all glo-ry seat-ed, King e-ter-nal, strong to save,
2. Thou art gone where now is giv-en What no mor-tal might could gain,
3. There Thy king-doms all a-dore Thee, Heav'n a-bove and earth be-low,
4. We, O Lord, with hearts a-dor-ing, Fol-low Thee a-bove the sky;

Dy-ing, Thou hast death de-feat-ed; Bur-ied, Thou hast spoil'd the grave!
On th' e-ter-nal throne of heav-en, In Thy Fa-ther's pow'r to reign.
While the depths of hell be-fore Thee Trembling and de-feat-ed bow.
Hear our pray'rs Thy grace im-plor-ing, Lift our souls to Thee on high. A-MEN.

73 O all ye works of the Lord!

O ALL, etc. | bless ye the Lord: PRAISE HIM, AND MAG-NI-FY HIM FOR EVER!

1 O All ye Works of the Lord, | bless ye the Lord: PRAISE HIM, etc.
3 O ye Sun and Moon, | bless ye the Lord: PRAISE HIM, etc.
5 O ye Winter and Summer, | bless ye the Lord: PRAISE HIM, etc.
7 O ye Mountains and all Hills, | bless ye the Lord: PRAISE HIM, etc.
9 O ye Kings of the earth and all Peoples, | bless ye the Lord: PRAISE HIM, etc.
11 O ye Spirits and Souls of the Righteous, | bless ye the Lord: PRAISE HIM, etc.

ADORATION OF CHRIST.

All hail the power of Jesus' name!

74

E. PERRONET, 1779.   "LAUD."   J. B. DYKES.

1. All hail the pow'r of Je - sus' name! Let an - gels prostrate fall; Bring
2. Ye chos-en seed of Is - rael's race, Ye ransom'd from the fall; Hail
3. Let ev - ery kindred, ev - ery tribe, On this ter - res - trial ball, To
4. O that with yon-der sa - cred throng, We at His feet may fall; We'll

forth the roy - al di - a - dem, And crown Him Lord of all!
Him, who saves you by His grace, And crown Him Lord of all!
Him all maj - es - ty as - cribe, And crown Him Lord of all!
join the ev - er - last - ing song, And crown Him Lord of all! A-MEN.

O all ye works of the Lord!—*Concluded.*

O ye, etc. | bless ye the Lord: PRAISE HIM, AND MAG-NI-FY HIM FOR EVER! A-MEN.

2 O ye Angels of the Lord, | bless ye the Lord: PRAISE HIM, etc,
4 O ye Stars of Heav'n, | bless ye the Lord: PRAISE HIM, etc.
6 O ye Nights and Days, | bless ye the Lord: PRAISE HIM, etc.
8 O ye Heights and Depths, | bless ye the Lord: PRAISE HIM, etc.
10 O ye Servants of the Lord, | bless ye the Lord: PRAISE HIM, etc.
12 O ye holy Men and humble of heart, | bless ye the Lord: PRAISE HIM, etc.

ADORATION OF CHRIST

79 When morning gilds the skies.

German, 17th Century.   H. F. SHEPPARD.

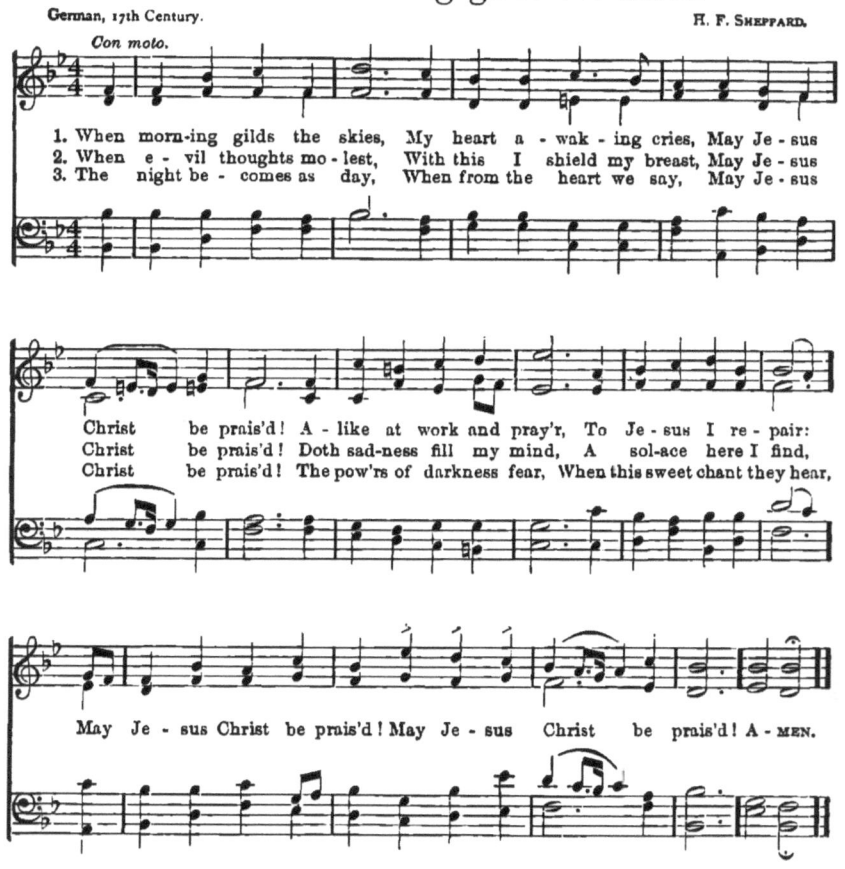

1. When morn-ing gilds the skies, My heart a-wak-ing cries, May Jesus Christ be prais'd! A-like at work and pray'r, To Je-sus I re-pair:
2. When e-vil thoughts mo-lest, With this I shield my breast, May Jesus Christ be prais'd! Doth sad-ness fill my mind, A sol-ace here I find,
3. The night be-comes as day, When from the heart we say, May Jesus Christ be prais'd! The pow'rs of darkness fear, When this sweet chant they hear,

May Je-sus Christ be prais'd! May Je-sus Christ be prais'd! A-MEN.

4 In heav'n's eternal bliss,
  The loveliest strain is this,
    May Jesus Christ be prais'd!
  Let earth and sea and sky
  From depth to height reply,
    May Jesus Christ be prais'd!

5 Be this, while life is mine,
  My canticle divine,
    May Jesus Christ be prais'd!
  Be this th'eternal song
  Down through the ages long,
    May Jesus Christ be prais'd! AMEN.

81. Singing for Jesus.

ADORATION OF CHRIST.

F. R. HAVERGAL. "BROMHAM." T. R. MATTHEWS, 1886.

1. Singing for Jesus, our Saviour and King, Singing for Jesus, the Lord whom we love; All adoration we joyously bring, Longing to praise as they praise Him above.
2. Singing for Jesus, and trying to win Many to love Him, and join in the song; Calling the weary and wandering in, Rolling the chorus of gladness along. AMEN.

3 Singing for Jesus, our Shepherd and Guide,
Singing for gladness of heart that He gives;
Singing for wonder and praise that He died,
Singing for blessing and joy that He lives.

4 Singing for Jesus, yes, singing for joy;
Thus will we praise Him and tell out His love,
Till He shall call us to brighter employ,
Singing for Jesus, for ever above. AMEN.

ADORATION OF CHRIST.

Saviour, blessed Saviour.

82

G. Thring, 1862.   "PRINCETHORPE."   W. Pitts.

1. Saviour, bless-ed Saviour, List-en while we sing; Hearts and voi-ces rais-ing Prais-es to our King. All we have we of-fer, All we hope to be, Bod-y, soul, and spir-it, All we yield to Thee.

2. Near-er, ev-er near-er, Christ, we draw to Thee, Deep in ad-o-ra-tion Bend-ing low the knee. Thou for our re-demp-tion, Cam'st on earth to die; Thou, that we might fol-low, Hast gone up on high. A-MEN.

3 Clearer still, and clearer
   Dawns the light from heaven;
In our sadness bringing
   News of sin forgiven.
Life has lost its shadows,
   Pure the light within;
Thou hast shed Thy radiance
   On a world of sin.

4 Higher then, and higher,
   Bear the ransom'd soul,
Earthly toils forgetting,
   Saviour, to its goal;
Where, in joys unthought of,
   Saints with angels sing,
Never weary, raising
   Praises to their King. AMEN.

83 — ADORATION OF CHRIST.

Crown Him with many crowns.

M. BRIDGES, 1847. "DIADEMATA." G. J. ELVEY.

1. Crown Him with man-y crowns, The Lamb up-on His throne! Hark, how the heav'nly an-them drowns All mu-sic but its own! A-wake, my soul, and sing Of Him who died for thee; And hail Him as thy matchless King Thro' all e-ter-ni-ty.
2. Crown Him the Lord of love! Be-hold His hands and side,—Dear wounds, yet vis-i-ble a-bove, In beau-ty glo-ri-fied. No an-gel in the sky Can ful-ly bear the sight, But downward bends his wond'ring eye At myster-ies so bright. A-MEN.

3 Crown Him the Lord of peace!
  Whose pow'r a sceptre sways
From pole to pole, that wars may cease,
  And all be pray'r and praise.
His reign shall know no end;
  And round His pierced feet
Fair flow'rs of Paradise extend
  Their fragrance ever sweet

4 Crown Him the Lord of years,
  The Potentate of time,
Creator of the rolling spheres,
  Ineffably sublime!
All hail, Redeemer, hail!
  For Thou hast died for me;
Thy praise shall never, never fail
  Throughout eternity! AMEN.

ADORATION OF CHRIST.

O who like Thee, so calm, so bright.

A. C. COXE. "ST. BASIL." German.
Stately.

1. O who like Thee, so calm, so bright, Thou Son of Man, Thou Light of Light!
2. And all Thy life's un-chang-ing years, A man of sor-rows and of tears,
3. O wondrous Lord, our souls would be Still more and more con-form'd to Thee,

O who like Thee did ev - er go So pa-tient thro' a world of woe!
The cross, where all our sins were laid, Up - on Thy bending shoulders weigh'd;
And learn of Thee, the low - ly One, And like Thee all our jour-ney run.

O who like Thee so hum - bly bore The scorn, the scoffs of men be-fore;—
And death, that sets the pris-'ner free, Was pang and scoff and scorn to Thee;
O in this light be ours to go, Il - lu-ming ev - ery way of woe;

So meek, for - giv - ing, God-like, high, So glorious in hu - mil - i - ty!
Yet love thro' all Thy tor - ture glow'd, And mer - cy with Thy life-blood flow'd.
And give us ev - er on the road To trace Thy footsteps, Son of God. A-MEN.

ADORATION OF CHRIST.

87 Jesus, the very thought of Thee.

Latin, 12th Century.   R. REDHEAD, 1872.

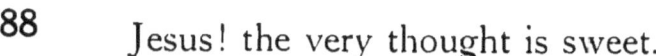

1. Je - sus, the ve - ry thought of Thee, With sweetness fills my breast; But
2. Nor voice can sing, nor heart can frame, Nor can the mem - 'ry find A
3. O hope of ev - ery con - trite heart! O joy of all the meek! To

sweet - er far Thy face to see, And in Thy pres-ence rest.
sweet - er sound than Thy blest name, O Sav-iour of man-kind.
those who fall, how kind Thou art, How good to those who seek! A-MEN.

4 But what to those who find? Ah, this
   Nor tongue nor pen can show;
   The love of Jesus—what it is
   None but His lov'd ones know.

5 Jesus, our only joy be Thou,
   As Thou our crown wilt be;
   Jesus, be Thou our glory now,
   And through eternity. AMEN.

88 Jesus! the very thought is sweet.

Latin, 12th Century.   "CANONBURY."   R. SCHUMANN.

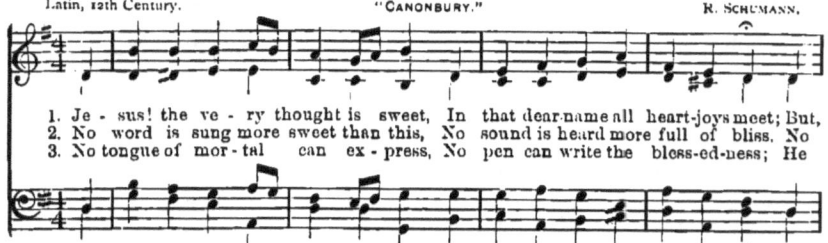

1. Je - sus! the ve - ry thought is sweet, In that dear name all heart-joys meet; But,
2. No word is sung more sweet than this, No sound is heard more full of bliss. No
3. No tongue of mor - tal can ex - press, No pen can write the bless-ed-ness; He

4 O Jesus, King of wondrous might!
   O Victor, glorious from the fight!
   Sweetness that may not be express'd,
   And altogether loveliest!

ADORATION OF CHRIST

The King of love my Shepherd is.

H. W. BAKER, 1868.   "DOMINUS REGIT ME."   J. B. DYKES, 1868.

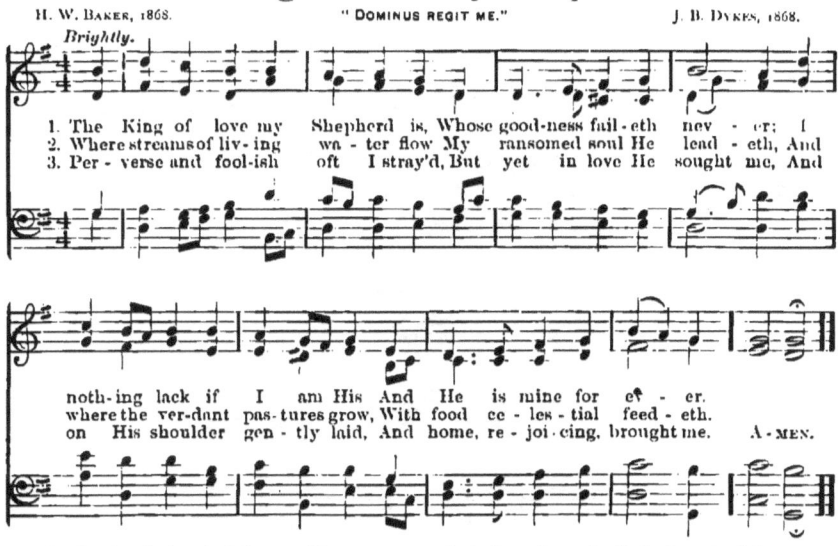

1. The King of love my Shepherd is, Whose goodness faileth never; I nothing lack if I am His And He is mine for ever.
2. Where streams of living water flow My ransomed soul He leadeth, And where the verdant pastures grow, With food celestial feedeth.
3. Perverse and foolish oft I stray'd, But yet in love He sought me, And on His shoulder gently laid, And home, rejoicing, brought me. A-MEN.

4 In death's dark vale I fear no ill
With Thee, dear Lord, beside me,
Thy rod and staff my comfort still,
Thy cross before to guide me.

5 And so through all the length of days
Thy goodness faileth never;
Good Shepherd, may I sing Thy praise
Within Thy house for ever. AMEN.

Jesus! the very thought is sweet.—*Concluded.*

O! than honey sweeter far   The glimpses of His presence are.
thought brings sweeter comfort nigh, Than Jesus, Son of God most High.
only who hath prov'd it knows What bliss from love of Jesus flows. A-MEN.

5 Abide with us, O Lord, to-day;
Fulfil us with Thy grace, we pray;
And with Thine own true sweetness feed
Our souls, from sin and darkness freed. AMEN.

ADORATION

90   Glory be to God on high! (I.)
"Gloria in Excelsis."

Latin, 3d or 4th Century.   *PARTS I & III.*   W. Crotch.

1 Glory be to | God on | high; ||
    And on earth | peace, good- | will toward | men.
3 O Lord God, | heav'n-ly | King, ||
    God the | Fa-ther Al- | mighty.
8 For Thou | only art | holy; ||
    Thou | on-ly art the | Lord;

2 We praise Thee, we bless Thee, we | wor-ship | Thee, ||
    We glorify Thee, we give thanks to | Thee for | Thy great | glory.
4 O Lord, the only begotten Son, | Je-sus | Christ; ||
    O Lord God, Lamb of | God, Son | of the | Father;
9 Thou only, O Christ, with the | Ho-ly | Ghost, |
    Art most high in the glory of | God the | Father: A- | men.

PART II.   J. T. Cooper.

5 That takest away the | sin · of the | world, ||
    Have | mer- | cy up- | on us:
6 Thou that takest away the | sin · of the | world, ||
    Re- | ceive | our | prayer:
7 Thou that sittest on the right hand of | God the | Father, ||
    Have | mer- | cy up- | on us.
    [8th and 9th verses above.]

In singing this and the following chant, care should be taken to follow the order of the verses as indicated by their numbers.

ADORATION.

Glory be to God on high! (II.)
"Gloria in Excelsis."

[SECOND TUNE.]   *PARTS I & IV.*   Traditional.

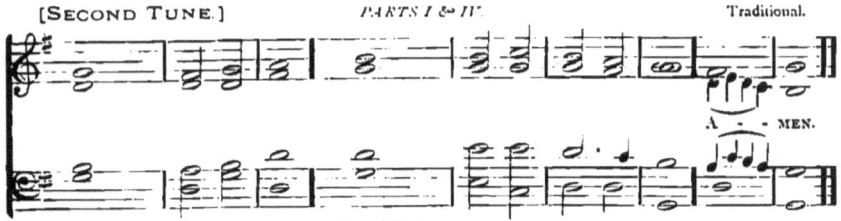

1 Glory be to | God on | high;‖
   And on earth | peace, good- | will toward | men.
2 We praise Thee, we bless Thee, we | wor-ship | Thee,‖
   We glorify Thee, we give thanks to | Thee for | Thy great | glory,
3 For Thou | only art | holy;‖
   Thou | on-ly | art the | Lord:
9 Thou only, O Christ, with the | Ho-ly | Ghost,‖
   Art most high in the | glory of | God the | Father: ‖A-men.‖

PART II.

3 O Lord God, heav'n-ly | King,‖
   God the | Fa-ther | Al- | mighty.
4 O Lord, the only begotten Son, | Je-sus | Christ;‖
   O Lord God, Lamb of | God, Son | of the | Father;

PART III.

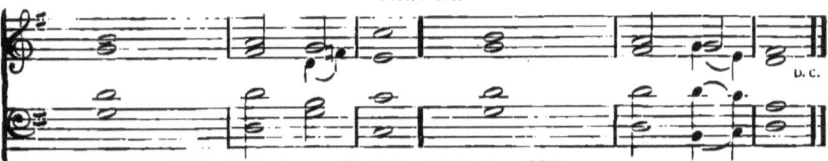

5 That takest away the | sin - of the | world,‖
   Have | mercy up- on us:
6 Thou that takest away the | sin - of the | world,‖
   Re- ceive our | prayer:
7 Thou that sittest at the right hand of | God the | Father, ‖
   Have | mercy up- | on us.
   [8th and 9th verses above.]

91. Glory be to the Father! (I.)

ADORATION.

Latin, 2d century.   "GLORIA PATRI."   H. LAWES.

1 Glory be to the Father, | and • to the | Son, ||
   And | to the | Ho-ly | Ghost:

2 As it was in the beginning, is now, and | ev-er | shall be, ||
   World | with-out | end: A- | MEN.

91ª. Glory be to the Father! (II.)

"GLORIA PATRI."   G. A. MACFARREN.

1 Glory be to the Father, | and • to the | Son, ||
   And | to the | Ho-ly | Ghost:

2 As it was in the beginning, is now, and | ev-er | shall be, ||
   World | with-out | end: A- | MEN

Songs of Thanksgiving.

My God, I thank Thee.   92

Miss A. A. Proctor.   "Wentworth."   F. C. Maker.
Con moto.

1. My God, I thank Thee, who hast made The earth so bright,
2. I thank Thee too that Thou hast made Joy to a-bound;
3. I thank Thee, Lord, that Thou hast kept The best in store;
4. I thank Thee, Lord, that here our souls, Though amp-ly blest,

So full of splen-dor and of joy, Beau-ty and light;
So ma-ny gen-tle thoughts and deeds Circ-ling us round;
I have e-nough, yet not too much To long for more,—
Can nev-er find, al-though they seek, A per-fect rest,—

So ma-ny glo-rious things are here, No-ble and right.
That in the dark-est spot of earth Some love is found.
A yearn-ing for a deep-er peace Not known be-fore.
Nor ev-er shall, un-til they lean On Je-sus' breast. A-men.

THANKSGIVING.

Lord, with glowing heart I'd praise Thee.

F. S. Key, 1826.   "St. Chad."   R. Redhead.

Andante.

1. Lord, with glow-ing heart I'd praise Thee For the bliss Thy love be-stows,
2. Praise, my soul, the God that sought thee, Wretched wand'rer, far a-stray;
3. Lord, this bo-som's ar-dent feel-ing Vain-ly would my lips ex-press;

For the pard'ning grace that saves me, And the peace that from it flows.
Found thee lost, and kind-ly brought thee From the paths of death a-way:
Low be-fore Thy foot-stool kneel-ing, Deign Thy suppliant's pray'r to bless.

UNISON

Help, O God, my weak en-deav-or, This dull soul to rap-ture raise;
Praise, with love's de-vout-est feel-ing, Him who saw thy guilt-born fear,
Let Thy grace, my soul's chief treas-ure, Love's pure flame with-in me raise;

Thou must light the flame, or nev-er Can my love be warm'd to praise.
And, the light of hope re-veal-ing, Bade the blood-stain'd cross appear.
And since words can nev-er meas-ure, Let my life show forth Thy praise. A-MEN.

THANKSGIVING.

For all Thy care we bless Thee.—*Concluded.*

3 For all Thy truth we bless Thee;
　Our human vows are frail,
　But through the strife of ages
　　Thy word can never fail.
　The kingdoms shall be broken,
　　The mighty ones shall fall;
　The promise Thou hast spoken
　　Shall triumph over all.

4 O teach us how to praise Thee,
　And touch our hearts with fire!
　O let the Spirit's presence
　　Our hearts and minds inspire!
　Thus toiling, watching, singing,
　　We tread our earthly way,
　While every hour is bringing
　　Nearer the dawn of day.　AMEN.

O Lord of heaven and earth and sea.　96

C. WORDSWORTH, 1862.　　　　　　　　　　　　　　　　S. S. WESLEY.

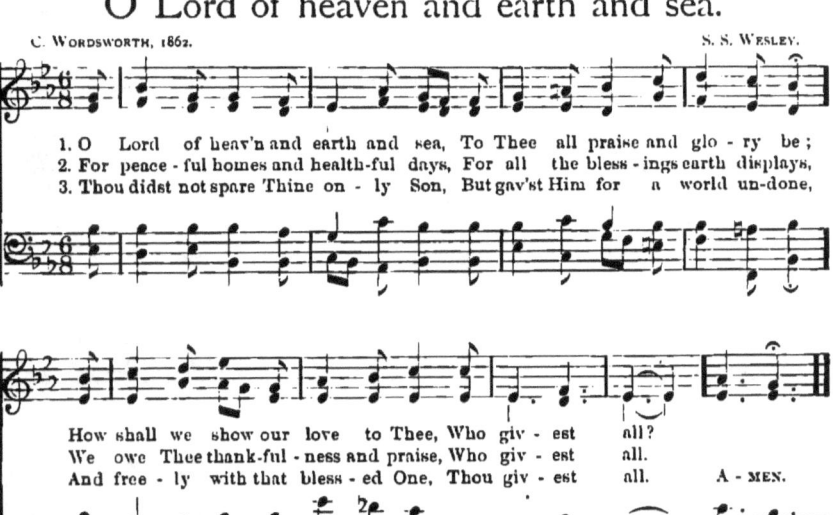

1. O Lord of heav'n and earth and sea, To Thee all praise and glo-ry be;
2. For peace-ful homes and health-ful days, For all the bless-ings earth displays,
3. Thou didst not spare Thine on-ly Son, But gav'st Him for a world un-done,

How shall we show our love to Thee, Who giv-est all?
We owe Thee thank-ful-ness and praise, Who giv-est all.
And free-ly with that bless-ed One, Thou giv-est all.　A-MEN.

4 Thou giv'st the Holy Spirit's dower,
　Spirit of life, and love, and power,
　And dost His sevenfold graces shower,
　　Upon us all.

5 For souls redeem'd, for sins forgiven,
　For means of grace, and hopes of heaven
　Father, what can to Thee be given,
　　Who givest all?

6 Whatever, Lord, we lend to Thee,
　Repaid a thousandfold will be;
　Then gladly will we give to Thee,
　　Who givest all;—

7 To Thee, from whom we all derive
　Our life, our gifts, our power to give;
　Oh, may we ever for Thee live,
　　Who givest all.　AMEN.

THANKSGIVING.

97. Sing to the Lord a joyful song.

J. S. B. Monsell, 1863.
Con moto.
J. Barnby, 1872.

1. Sing to the Lord a joy-ful song, Lift up your hearts, your voi-ces raise;
2. For life and love, for rest and food, For dai-ly help and night-ly care,
3. For joys un-told that from a-bove Cheer those who love His sweet em-ploy,
4. For life be-low, with all its bliss, And for that life, more pure and high,

To us His gra-cious gifts be-long, To Him our songs of love and praise.
Sing to the Lord, for He is good, And praise His name, for it is fair!
Sing to our God, for He is love; Ex-alt His name for it is joy!
That in-ner life, which o-ver this Shall ev-er shine, and nev-er die,

REFRAIN.

Sing to the Lord of heav'n and earth, Whom an-gels serve and saints a-dore,

The Fa-ther, Son, and Ho-ly Ghost, To whom be praise for ev-er-more! A-MEN.

100. For the beauty of the earth.

THANKSGIVING.

F. S. PIERPOINT, 1864.   "LILYBOURNE."   S. SMITH, 1886.

1. For the beau-ty of the earth, For the glo-ry of the skies,
For the love which from our birth O-ver and a-round us lies,
Lord of all, to Thee we raise This our hymn of grate-ful praise. A-MEN.

2. For the won-der of each hour Of the day and of the night,
Hill and vale, and tree and flower, Sun and moon, and stars of light,

3 For the joy of human love,
  Brother, sister, parent, child,
  Friends on earth, and friends above,
  Pleasures pure and undefil'd,
    Lord of all, to Thee we raise
    This our hymn of grateful praise.

4 For the Church that evermore
  Lifteth holy hands above,
  Off'ring up on every shore
  Her pure sacrifice of love,
    Lord of all, to Thee we raise
    This our hymn of grateful praise. AMEN.

THANKSGIVING.

Summer suns are glowing. 101

W. W. How. "RUTH." S. SMITH.
Brightly.

1. Summer suns are glow-ing O - ver land and sea, Hap-py light is flow-ing Boun - ti - ful and free. Ev - ery - thing re - joic - es In the mel - low rays, And earth's thousand voi - ces Swell the psalm of praise.

2. God's free mercy streameth O - ver all the world, And His ban-ner gleameth Ev - ry-where un-furl'd. Broad and deep and glo-rious, As the heav'n a - bove, Shines in might vic - to - rious His e - ter - nal love. A - MEN.

3 Lord, upon our blindness
    Thy pure radiance pour;
For Thy loving-kindness
    Make us love Thee more.
And when clouds are drifting
    Dark across our sky,
Then, the veil uplifting,
    Father, be Thou nigh.

4 We will never doubt Thee,
    Though Thou veil Thy light;
Life is dark without Thee:
    Death with Thee is bright.
Light of Light! shine o'er us
    On our pilgrim-way,
Go Thou still before us
    To the endless day. AMEN.

THANKSGIVING.

102 I will extol Thee, my God, O King!

From Psalm 145.   H. Smart.

1 I will extol Thee, my | God, O | King, ||
   And I will bless Thy | name for | ever and | ever.

3 The Lord is good to all, and His tender mercies are over | all His | works: ||
   All Thy works shall give thanks unto Thee, O Lord, and Thy | saints shall | bless | Thee.

5 The Lord is righteous in | all His | ways, ||
   And | gracious in | all His | works.

7 Glory be to the Father, | and • to the | Son, ||
   And | to the | Holy | Ghost;

---

103 It is a good thing to give thanks.

From Psalm 92   "Bonum est confiteri."   J. L. Hopkins.

1 It is a good thing to give thanks | unto the | Lord,
   And to sing praises unto | Thy name, | O Most | High;

3 With an instrument of ten strings, | and • with the | psaltery,
   With a solemn | sound up- | on the | harp.

5 How great are Thy works, O Lord! Thy thoughts are | very deep,
   Thou, O Lord, art on | high for | ever- | more.

7 Glory be to the Father, | and • to the | Son,
   And to the | Holy | Ghost;

THANKSGIVING.

I will extol Thee, my God, O King.—*Concluded.*

2 Every | day • will I | bless Thee, ||
   And I will praise Thy | name for | ever and ever.

4 The eyes of all wait upon Thee, and Thou givest them their | food • in due | season; ||
   Thou openest Thy hand, and satisfiest the desire of | every | living | thing.

6 The Lord is nigh unto all them that | call up- | on Him, ||
   To all that | call upon | Him in | truth.

8 As it was in the beginning, is now, and | ever | shall be, ||
   World | without | end: A- | MEN.

It is a good thing to give thanks.—*Concluded.*

2 To show forth Thy loving kindness | in the | morning,
   And Thy faithfulness | every | night.

4 For Thou, Lord, hast made me | glad • through Thy | work;
   I will triumph in the | works of | Thy | hands.

6 For lo, Thine enemies, O Lord, Thine enemies | shall | perish;
   All the workers of in- iquity | shall be | scatter'd.

8 As it was in the beginning, is now, and | ever | shall be
   World | without | end: A- | MEN.

Songs to the Holy Spirit.

Creator Spirit, by whose aid.

1. Cre - a - tor Spir - it, by whose aid The world's founda - tions first were laid,
2. O source of un - cre - a - ted light, The Fa - ther's promis'd Pa - ra - clete,
3. Plenteous of grace, de - scend from high, Rich in Thy seven-fold en - er - gy;

Come, vis - it ev - ery hum - ble mind; Come, pour Thy joys on hu - man - kind;
Thrice ho - ly Fount, thrice ho - ly Fire, Our hearts with heav'n - ly love in - spire;
Make us e - ter - nal truths re - ceive, And prac - tice all that we be - lieve;

From sin and sor - row set us free, And make Thy temples worth - y Thee.
Come, and Thy sa - cred unction bring To sanc - ti - fy us while we sing.
Give us Thyself, that we may see The Fa - ther and the Son by Thee. A-MEN.

106 Come Thou, O come.

HOLY SPIRIT.

Latin, 9th Century. "HURSTMONCEUX." E. PROUT, 1887.
Slowly and tenderly.

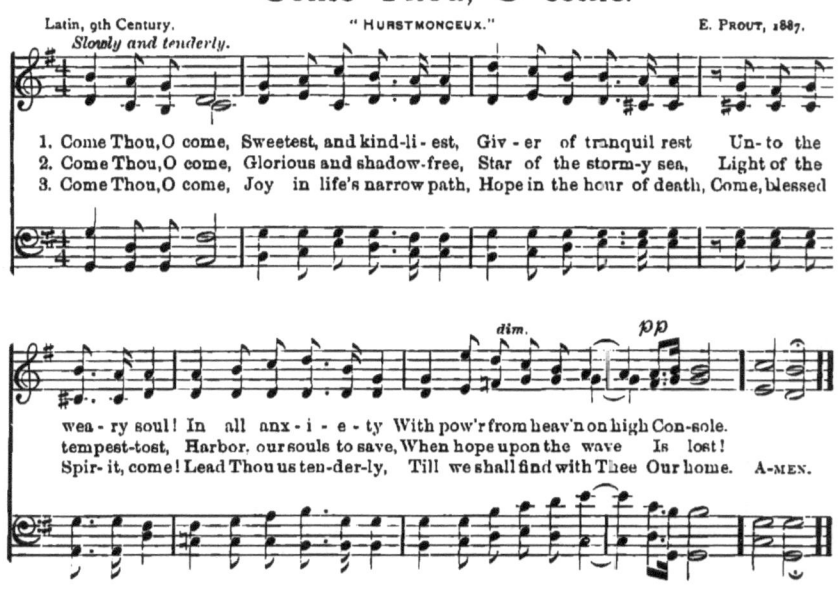

1. Come Thou, O come, Sweetest, and kind-li-est, Giv-er of tranquil rest Un-to the wea-ry soul! In all anx-i-e-ty With pow'r from heav'n on high Con-sole.
2. Come Thou, O come, Glorious and shadow-free, Star of the storm-y sea, Light of the tempest-tost, Harbor our souls to save, When hope upon the wave Is lost!
3. Come Thou, O come, Joy in life's narrow path, Hope in the hour of death, Come, blessed Spir-it, come! Lead Thou us ten-der-ly, Till we shall find with Thee Our home. A-MEN.

107 Come, Holy Spirit, come!

J. HART, 1759. "CHISELHURST." J. BARNBY, 1887.
Con brio.

1. Come, Ho-ly Spir-it, come! Let Thy bright beams a - rise; Dis-pel the
2. Re - vive our droop-ing faith, Our doubts and fears re - move, And kin-dle
3. Dwell therefore in our hearts, Our minds from bondage free; Then shall we

HOLY SPIRIT. 108

Holy Spirit, Truth divine.

S. LONGFELLOW.   "SEYMOUR."   C. M. VON WEBER, 1826.

Cantabile.

1. Ho - ly Spir - it, Truth di - vine, Dawn up - on this soul of mine;
2. Ho - ly Spir - it, Love di - vine, Glow with - in this heart of mine;
3. Ho - ly Spir - it, Pow'r di - vine, Fill and nerve this will of mine;

Word of God, and in - ward Light, Wake my spir - it, clear my sight.
Kin - dle ev - ery high de - sire; Per - ish self in Thy pure fire!
By Thee may I strong - ly live, Brave - ly bear, and no - bly strive. A-MEN.

4 Holy Spirit, Peace divine,
  Still this restless heart of mine;
  Speak to calm this tossing sea,
  Stay'd in Thy tranquillity.

5 Holy Spirit, Joy divine,
  Gladden Thou this heart of mine;
  In the desert-ways I sing,
  "Spring, O Well, for ever spring!" AMEN.

Come, Holy Spirit, come!—*Concluded.*

dark - ness from our minds, And o - pen all our eyes.
in our breasts the flame Of nev - er - dy - ing love.
know, and praise, and love, The Fa - ther, Son, and Thee. A-MEN.

109. Spirit blest, who art ador'd.

HOLY SPIRIT.

T. B. POLLOCK. H. P. MAIN, 1886.

1. Spirit blest, who art a-dor'd With the Father and the Word, One eternal God and Lord: Hear us, Holy Spirit. Holy Spirit, heav'nly Dove, Dew descending from above, Breath of life, and fire of love: Hear us, Holy Spirit.
2. Source of strength and knowledge clear, Wisdom, godliness sincere, Understanding, counsel, fear: Hear us, Holy Spirit. Source of meekness, love, and peace, Patience, pureness, faith's increase, Hope and joy that can not cease: Hear us, Holy Spirit.
3. All Thy sev'n-fold gifts bestow, Gifts of wisdom God to know, Gifts of strength to meet the foe: Hear us, Holy Spirit. Come, to strengthen all the weak, Give Thy courage to the meek, Teach our falt'ring tongues to speak: Hear us, Holy Spirit.
4. Come to aid the souls who yearn More of truth divine to learn, And with deeper love to burn: Hear us, Holy Spirit. Holy, loving, as Thou art, Come, and live within our heart, Never from us to depart: Hear us, Holy Spirit. A-MEN.

Copyright, 1897, by The Century Co.

111
Come, O Creator Spirit blest.

HOLY SPIRIT

Latin, 9th Century.   "LITLINGTON TOWER."   J. BARNBY, 1862.

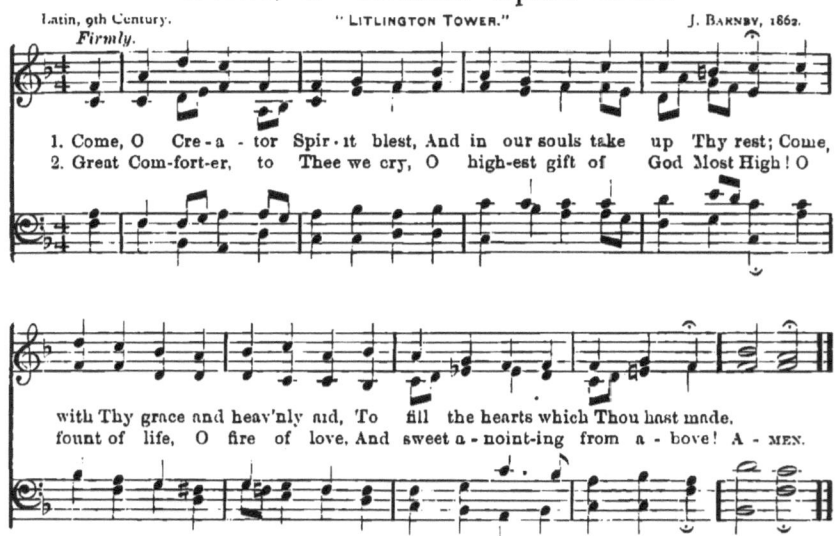

1. Come, O Cre-a-tor Spir-it blest, And in our souls take up Thy rest; Come, with Thy grace and heav'nly aid, To fill the hearts which Thou hast made.
2. Great Com-fort-er, to Thee we cry, O high-est gift of God Most High! O fount of life, O fire of love, And sweet a-noint-ing from a-bove! A-MEN.

3 Our senses touch with light and fire,
Our hearts with charity inspire;
And with endurance from on high
The weakness of our flesh supply.

4 Far back our enemy repel,
And let Thy peace within us dwell;
So may we, having Thee for Guide,
Turn from each hurtful thing aside. AMEN.

112
Our blest Redeemer, ere He breathed.

Miss H. AUBER, 1829.   "ST. CUTHBERT."   J. B. DYKES, 1861.

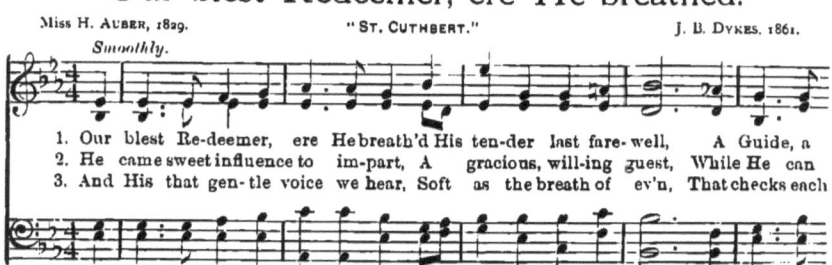

1. Our blest Re-deemer, ere He breath'd His ten-der last fare-well, A Guide, a
2. He came sweet influence to im-part, A gracious, will-ing guest, While He can
3. And His that gen-tle voice we hear, Soft as the breath of ev'n, That checks each

HOLY SPIRIT

Come, gracious Spirit, heavenly Dove. 113

S. BROWNE, 1720.   W. HARRISON.
Andante.

1. Come, gracious Spir - it, heav'n - ly Dove, With light and com-fort from a - bove;
2. The light of truth to us dis - play, And make us know and love Thy way;

Be Thou our Guardian, Thou our Guide, O'er every thought and step pre-side.
Plant ho-ly fear in ev - ery heart, That we from God may ne'er de - part. A - MEN.

3 Lead us to holiness, the road
   That we must take to dwell with God;
   Lead us to Christ, the living Way,
   Nor let us from His precepts stray.

4 Lead us to God, our final Rest,
   To be with Him for ever blest;
   Lead us to heav'n, that we may share
   Fulness of joy for ever there. AMEN.

Our blest Redeemer.—*Concluded.*

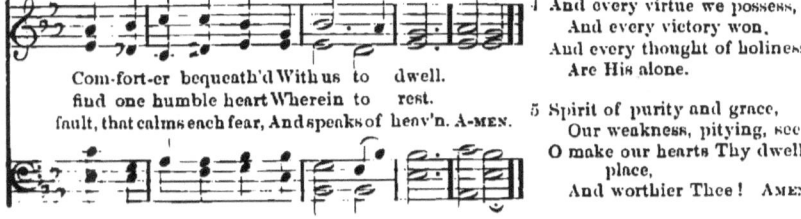

Com-fort-er bequeath'd With us to dwell.
find one humble heart Wherein to rest.
fault, that calms each fear, And speaks of heav'n. A-MEN.

4 And every virtue we possess,
   And every victory won,
   And every thought of holiness,
   Are His alone.

5 Spirit of purity and grace,
   Our weakness, pitying, see ;
   O make our hearts Thy dwelling-place,
   And worthier Thee ! AMEN.

HOLY SPIRIT

114. Come, Holy Ghost, in love.

Latin, 10th Century.   "PENTECOST."   G. Lomas.

1. Come, Holy Ghost, in love, Shed on us from above Thine own bright ray; Divinely good Thou art: Thy sacred gifts impart To gladden each sad heart; O come to-day!

2. Come, tend'rest Friend and best, Our most delightful Guest, With soothing pow'r,—Rest, which the weary know, Shade, 'mid the noontide glow, Peace, when deep griefs o'er-flow, Cheer us this hour. A-MEN.

3 Come, Light serene and still,
  Our inmost bosoms fill;
    Dwell in each breast;
We know no dawn but Thine;
Send forth Thy beams divine,
On our dark souls to shine,
    And make us blest.

4 Come, all the faithful bless;
  Let all who Christ confess
    His praise employ;
Give virtue's rich reward;
Victorious death accord,
And, with our glorious Lord,
    Eternal joy. AMEN.

Songs of Confession and Supplication.

No, not despairingly. 115

116 Rock of Ages, cleft for me.

CONFESSION.

A. M. TOPLADY, 1776.   "ROCK OF AGES."   R. REDHEAD, 1853.

1. Rock of A-ges, cleft for me, Let me hide my-self in Thee! Let the wa-ter and the blood, From Thy riv-en side which flow'd, Be of sin the doub-le cure, Cleanse me from its guilt and pow'r!

2. Not the la-bor of my hands Can ful-fil Thy law's de-mands; Could my zeal no re-spite know, Could my tears for ev-er flow,— All for sin could not a-tone; Thou must save, and Thou a-lone! A-MEN.

3 Nothing in my hand I bring,
Simply to Thy cross I cling;
Naked, come to Thee for dress:
Helpless, look to Thee for grace;
Foul, I to the fountain fly;
Wash me, Saviour, or I die!

4 While I draw this fleeting breath,
When my eyelids close in death,
When I soar to worlds unknown,
See Thee on Thy judgment-throne,
Rock of Ages, cleft for me,
Let me hide myself in Thee! AMEN.

CONFESSION.

O sacred Head, now wounded.

117

Latin, 12th Century.   "PASSION CHORALE."   German, 1601

1. { O sa - cred Head, now wound - ed, With grief and shame weigh'd down,
   { Now scorn - ful - ly sur - round - ed, With thorns, Thine on - ly crown,
2. { What Thou, my Lord, hast suf - fer'd Was all for sin - ners' gain:
   { Mine, mine was the trans - gres - sion, But Thine the dead - ly pain:

O sa - cred Head, what glo - ry, What bliss till now was Thine!
Lo, here I fall, my Sav - iour! 'Tis I de - serve Thy place;

Yet, tho' des-pis'd and go - ry, I joy to call Thee mine.
Look on me with Thy fa - vor, Vouch-safe to me Thy grace. A-MEN.

3 What language shall I borrow
  To thank Thee, dearest Friend,
For this, Thy dying sorrow,
  Thy pity without end?
Lord, make me Thine for ever,
  Nor let me faithless prove:
O let me never, never,
  Abuse such dying love!

4 Be near when I am dying,
  O show Thy cross to me;
And for my succor flying,
  Come, Lord, and set me free!
These eyes, new faith receiving,
  From Jesus shall not move;
For he who dies believing,
  Dies safely, through Thy love. AMEN.

CONFESSION

Lord Jesus, when we stand afar.

119

W. W. How, 1854.   "ST. VINCENT."   S. NEUKOMM.
Cantabile.

1. Lord Jesus, when we stand afar, And gaze upon Thy holy cross, In love of Thee and scorn of self, O may we count the world as loss.

2. When we behold Thy bleeding wounds, And the rough way that Thou hast trod, Make us to hate the load of sin That lay so heavy on our God. A-MEN.

3 O holy Lord, uplifted high,
  With outstretch'd arms, in mortal woe,
  Embracing in Thy wondrous love
  The sinful world that lies below,—

4 Give us an ever-living faith
  To gaze beyond the things we see;
  And in the myst'ry of Thy death
  Draw us and all men unto Thee. AMEN.

120. Out of the deep I call.

CONFESSION.
H. W. BAKER. "LANGTON." ANON.

1. Out of the deep I call To Thee, O Lord, to Thee; Before Thy throne of grace I fall; Be merciful to me.
2. Out of the deep I cry, The woeful deep of sin, Of evil done in days gone by, Of evil now within.
3. Lord, there is mercy now, As ever was, with Thee; Before Thy throne of grace I fall; Be merciful to me. A-MEN.

121. Gentle Jesus, meek and mild.

C. WESLEY, 1742. "NEW CALABAR." J. D. FARRER.

1. Gentle Jesus, meek and mild, Look upon a little child; Pity my simplicity; Suffer me to come to Thee.
2. Lamb of God, I look to Thee; Thou shalt my example be: Thou art gentle, meek, and mild: Thou wast once a little child. A-MEN.

3 Loving Jesus, gentle Lamb,
In Thy gracious hands I am;
Make me, Saviour, what Thou art:
Live Thyself within my heart.

4 I shall then show forth Thy praise,
Serve Thee all my happy days;
Then the world shall always see
Christ, the Holy Child, in me. AMEN.

CONFESSION.

125. O Jesus, Thou art standing.

W. W. How, 1854. "ST. HILDA." German.
Cantabile.

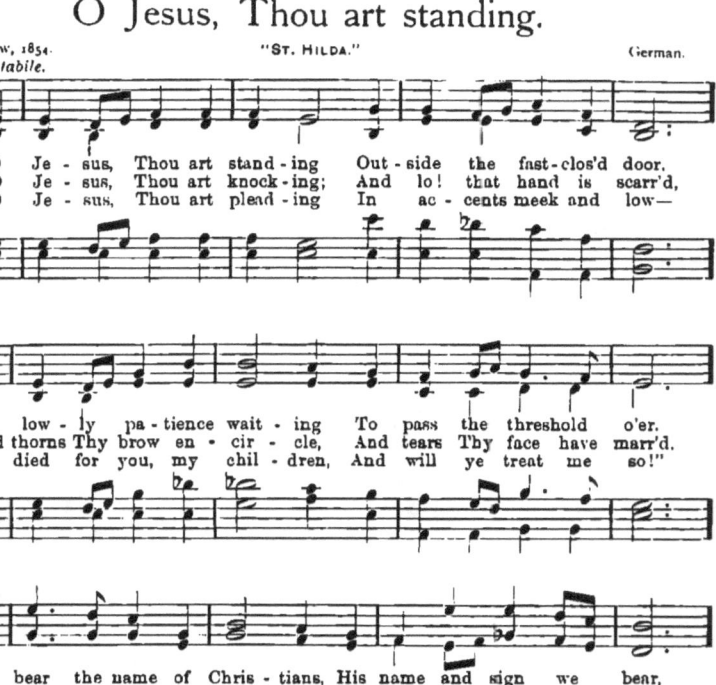

1. O Jesus, Thou art standing Outside the fast-clos'd door,
2. O Jesus, Thou art knocking; And lo! that hand is scarr'd,
3. O Jesus, Thou art pleading In accents meek and low—

In lowly patience waiting To pass the threshold o'er.
And thorns Thy brow encircle, And tears Thy face have marr'd.
"I died for you, my children, And will ye treat me so!"

We bear the name of Christians, His name and sign we bear,
O love that passeth knowledge, So patiently to wait!
O Lord, with shame and sorrow We open now the door;

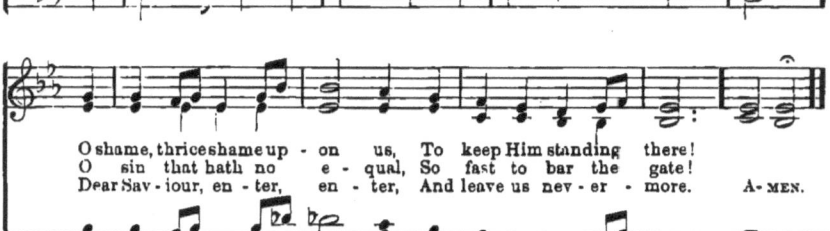

O shame, thrice shame upon us, To keep Him standing there!
O sin that hath no equal, So fast to bar the gate!
Dear Saviour, enter, enter, And leave us nevermore. A-MEN.

128. What grace, O Lord, and beauty shone.

SUPPLICATION FOR GRACE.

E. DENNY. "CALVARY." L. SPOHR, 1835.

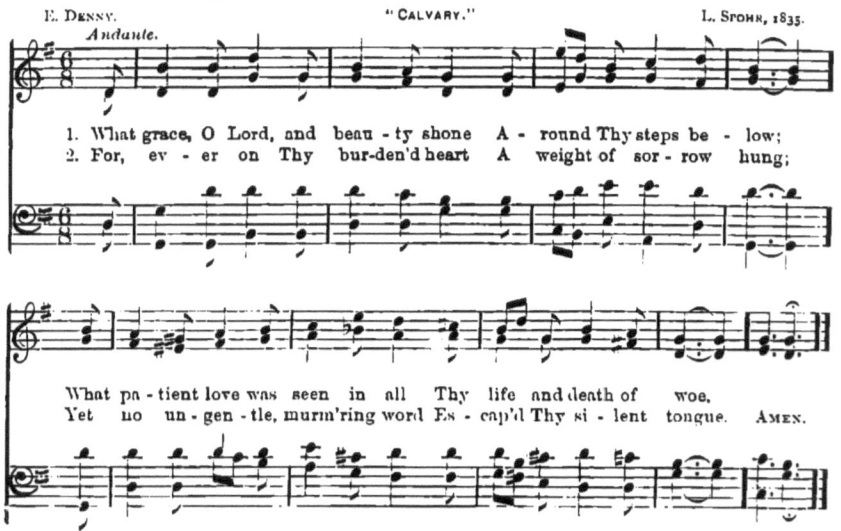

1. What grace, O Lord, and beau-ty shone A-round Thy steps be-low;
2. For, ev-er on Thy bur-den'd heart A weight of sor-row hung;

What pa-tient love was seen in all Thy life and death of woe.
Yet no un-gen-tle, murm'ring word Es-cap'd Thy si-lent tongue. AMEN.

3 O give us hearts to love like Thee,
Like Thee, O Lord, to grieve
Far more for others' sins, than all
The wrongs that we receive.

4 One with Thyself, may every eye,
In us, Thy brethren, see
The gentleness and grace that spring
From union, Lord, with Thee. AMEN.

129. When the world is brightest.

L. TUTTIETT. "PETROX." W. BOYD.

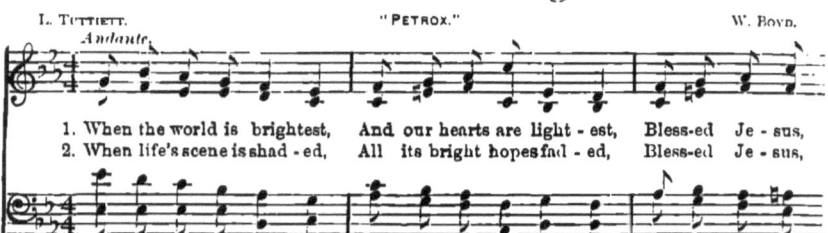

1. When the world is brightest, And our hearts are light-est, Bless-ed Je-sus,
2. When life's scene is shad-ed, All its bright hopes fad-ed, Bless-ed Je-sus,

SUPPLICATION FOR GRACE.

Grant us, O our Heavenly Father.

130

G. THRING.   "OSWALD."   J. B. DYKES.

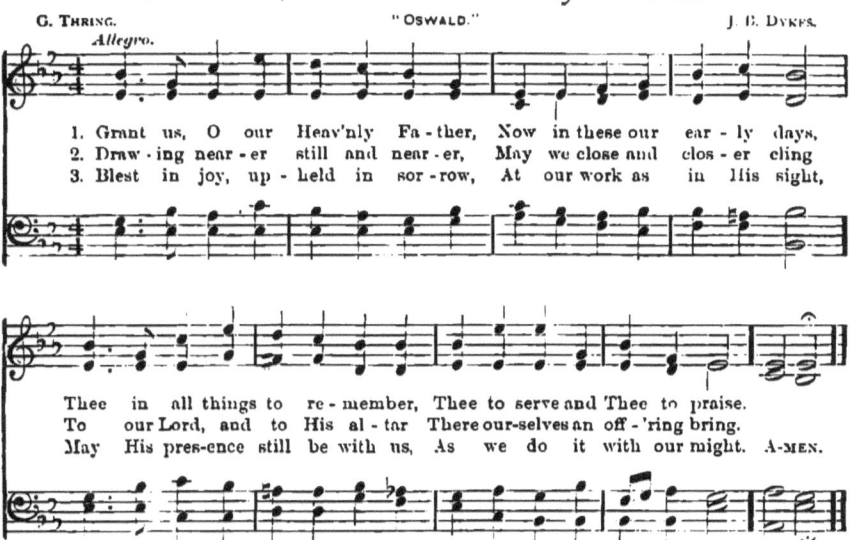

1. Grant us, O our Heav'nly Fa-ther, Now in these our ear-ly days,
2. Draw-ing near-er still and near-er, May we close and clos-er cling
3. Blest in joy, up-held in sor-row, At our work as in His sight,

Thee in all things to re-member, Thee to serve and Thee to praise.
To our Lord, and to His al-tar There our-selves an off-'ring bring.
May His pres-ence still be with us, As we do it with our might. A-MEN.

4 Serving Thee, our Heav'nly Father,
  From the dawn to set of sun,
  Serving Thee in life's young morning,
  Till our work on earth is done,—

5 Till the shadows of the evening
  Shall for ever pass away,
  And the Resurrection-morning
  Kindle into perfect day. AMEN.

When the world is brightest.—*Concluded.*

hear us! Let Thy hand be near us!
hear us! Light of heav'n, be near us! A-MEN.

3 When our foes surround us,
  When our sins have bound us,
  Blessed Jesus, hear us!
  Let Thy help be near us!

4 When life, slowly waning.
  Shows but heav'n remaining,
  Blessed Jesus, hear us!
  Light of all, be near us!
      AMEN.

SUPPLICATION FOR GRACE.

131. Come, Thou long-expected Jesus.

C. WESLEY, 1744.   "EXPECTATION."   F. MENDELSSOHN.

1. Come, Thou long-ex-pect-ed Je-sus, Born to set Thy peo-ple free; From our fears and sins re-lease us; Let us find our rest in Thee, Let us find our rest in Thee.
2. Is-rael's strength and con-so-la-tion, Hope of all the earth Thou art; Dear de-sire of ev-ery na-tion, Joy of ev-ery long-ing heart, Joy of ev-ery long-ing heart. A-MEN.

3 Born Thy people to deliver,
  Born a child and yet a King;
Born to reign in us for ever,
  Now Thy gracious kingdom bring.

4 By Thine own eternal Spirit,
  Rule in all our hearts alone;
By Thine all-sufficient merit,
  Raise us to Thy glorious throne. AMEN.

SUPPLICATION FOR GRACE.

Come, Jesus, Redeemer.

132

R. PALMER, 1867. A. E. FISHER, 1886.

1. Come, Je - sus, Re-deem - er, a - bide Thou with me; Come, glad - den my spir - it that wait - eth for Thee; Thy smile ev - ery shad - ow shall chase from my heart, And soothe ev - ery sor - row, tho' keen be the smart.

2. With - out Thee but weak - ness, with Thee I am strong; By day Thou shalt lead me, by night be my song; Tho' dan - gers sur - round me, I still ev - ery fear, Since Thou, the Most Mighty, my Help - er, art near.

3. Thy love, O how faith - ful! so ten - der, so pure! Thy prom - ise, faith's an - chor, how stead - fast and sure! That love, like sweet sun - shine, my cold heart can warm, That prom - ise make stead - y my soul in the storm. A-MEN.

4 Breathe, breathe on my spirit, oft ruffled, Thy peace;
From restless, vain wishes, bid Thou my heart cease;
In Thee all its longings henceforward shall end,
Till, glad, to Thy presence my soul shall ascend.

5 O then, blessed Jesus, who once for me died,
Made clean in the fountain that gush'd from Thy side,
I shall see thy full glory, Thy face shall behold,
And praise Thee with raptures for ever untold! AMEN.

Copyright, 1887, by The Century Co.

SUPPLICATION FOR GRACE.

133 Jesus, my Lord, my God, my All.

H. COLLINS, 1852. J. BARNBY, 1872.

1. Je-sus, my Lord, my God, my All, Hear me, blest Sav-iour, when I call,
2. Je-sus, too late I Thee have sought, How can I love Thee as I ought,
3. Je-sus, what didst Thou find in me That Thou hast dealt so lov-ing-ly?
4. Je-sus, of Thee shall be my song, To Thee my heart and soul be-long;

Hear me, and from Thy dwell-ing-place Pour down the rich - es of Thy grace.
And how ex - tol Thy match-less fame, The glo - rious beau - ty of Thy name?
How great the joy that Thou hast brought! O far ex - ceed - ing hope or thought!
All that I am or have is Thine; And Thou, my Sav - iour, Thou art mine.

Je-sus, my Lord, I Thee a - dore; O make me love Thee more and more. A-MEN.

134 Father, whate'er of earthly bliss.

Miss A. STEELE, 1760. H. J. GAUNTLETT.

1. Fa - ther, whate'er of earth-ly bliss Thy sov'reign will de - nies, Ac-
2. Give me a calm, a thank-ful heart, From ev - ery murmur free; The
3. Let the sweet hope that Thou art mine: My path of life at - tend; Thy

SUPPLICATION FOR GRACE.

Lord, in this Thy mercy's day. 135

I. Williams, 1844   "LACHRYMAE."   A. S. Sullivan.

1. Lord, in this Thy mer-cy's day, Ere from us it pass a-way, On our knees we fall and pray.
2. Lord, on us Thy Spir-it pour, Kneel-ing low-ly at the door, Ere it close for ev-er-more.
3. By Thy night of ag-o-ny, By Thy sup-pli-cat-ing cry, By Thy will-ing-ness to die; A-MEN.

4 By Thy tears of bitter woe
   For Jerusalem below,
   Let us not Thy love forego.

5 Judge and Saviour of our race,
   Grant us, when we see Thy face,
   With Thy ransom'd ones a place! AMEN.

Father, whate'er of earthly bliss.—*Concluded.*

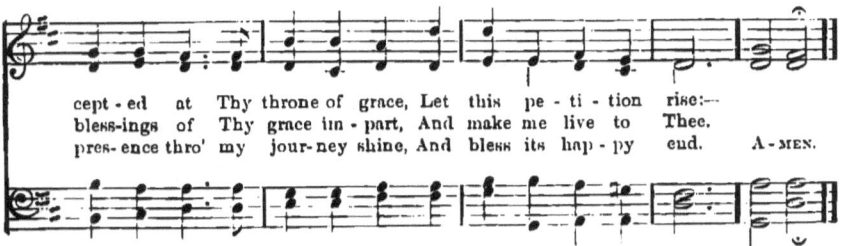

cept-ed at Thy throne of grace, Let this pe-ti-tion rise:—
bless-ings of Thy grace im-part, And make me live to Thee.
pres-ence thro' my jour-ney shine, And bless its hap-py end. A-MEN.

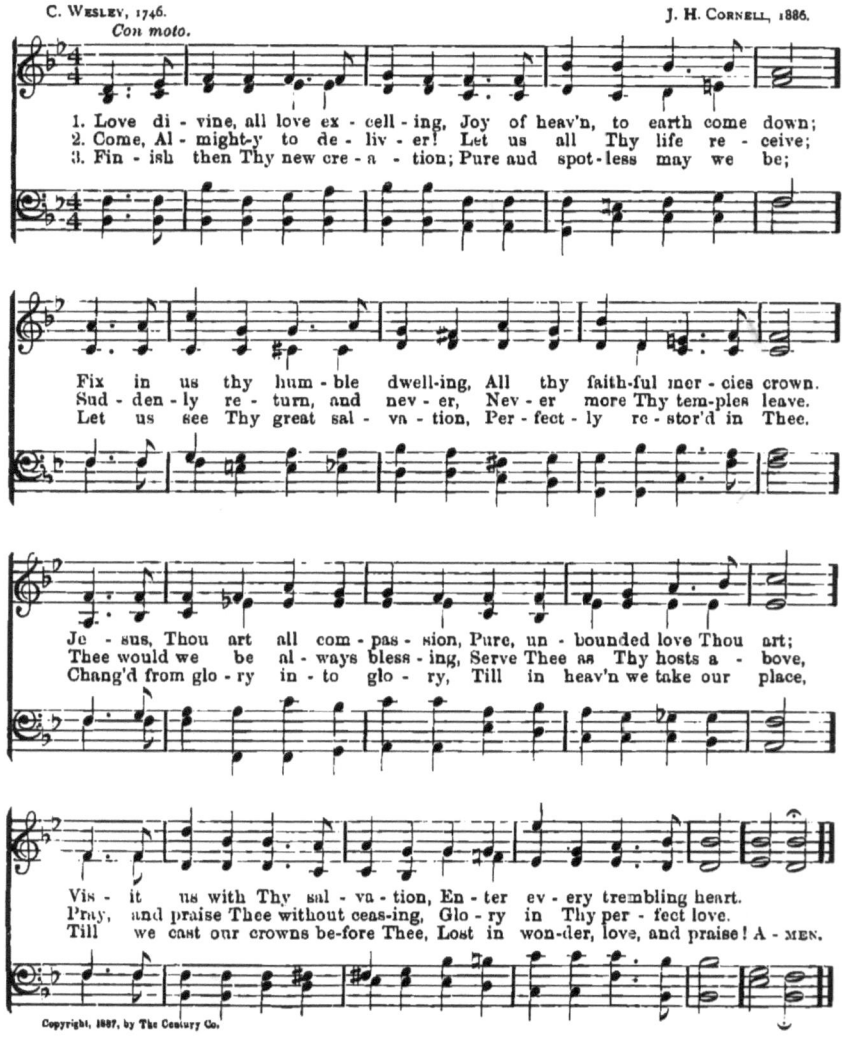

138. Father, hear Thy children's call.

SUPPLICATION FOR GRACE.

T. B. POLLOCK. *Expressively.* G. A. BURDETT, 1886.

1. Father, hear Thy children's call: Humbly at Thy feet we fall, Prodigals, confessing all: } We beseech Thee, hear us. A-MEN.
2. Love that caus'd us first to be, Love that bled upon the tree, Love that draws us lovingly:
3. We Thy call have disobey'd, Have neglected and delay'd, Into paths of sin have stray'd:
4. Hearing every contrite sigh, Bidding sinful souls draw nigh, Willing not that one should die:

5 Grant us faith to know Thee near,
   Hail Thy grace, Thy judgment fear,
   And through trial persevere:
     We beseech Thee, hear us.

6 Grant us hope from earth to rise,
   And to strain with eager eyes
   Tow'rds the promis'd heav'nly prize:
     We beseech Thee, hear us.

7 Grant us love Thy love to own,
   Love to live for Thee alone,
   And the pow'r of grace make known:
     We beseech Thee, hear us.

8 Lead us daily nearer Thee,
   Till at last Thy face we see,
   Crown'd with Thine own purity:
     We beseech Thee, hear us. AMEN.

Copyright, 1887, by The Century Co.

139. Our Father, who art in heaven.

From Matt. 6. THE LORD'S PRAYER. R. FARRANT.

1 Our Father, who art in heav'n, hallowed | be Thy | name; || Thy kingdom come; Thy will be done on | earth, as it | is in | heav'n;
2 Give us this day our | daily | bread; || And forgive us our trespasses, as we forgive | them that | trespass a- | gainst us; [... debts, as | we for- | give our | debtors;]
3 And lead us not into temptation, but deliver | us from | evil; || For Thine is the kingdom, and the pow'r, and the | glory, for | ever: A- | MEN.

SUPPLICATION FOR GRACE.

Saviour, teach me, day by day. 140

JANE E. LEESON, 1842.
Andante.
J. H. CORNELL, 1866.

Unison.
1. Sav-iour, teach me, day by day, Love's sweet les-son to o-bey; Sweet-er les-son can-not be, Lov-ing Him Who first lov'd me.
2. With a child-like heart of love, At Thy bid-ding may I move; Prompt to serve and fol-low Thee, Lov-ing Him Who first lov'd me.
3. Teach me all Thy steps to trace, Strong to fol-low in Thy grace; Learn-ing how to love from Thee, Lov-ing Him Who first lov'd me.
4. Thus may I re-joice to show That I feel the love I owe; Sing-ing, till Thy face I see, Of His love Who first lov'd me.

Copyright, 1886, by The Century Co.

Faithful Shepherd, feed me. 141

T. B. POLLOCK.
ANON, 1885.

1. Faith-ful Shepherd, feed me In the pastures green; Faithful Shepherd, lead me Where Thy steps are seen.
2. Hold me fast, and guide me In the nar-row way; So, with Thee be-side me, I shall nev-er stray.
3. Hal-low ev-ery pleas-ure, Ev-ery gift and pain; Be Thy-self my treas-ure, Tho' none else I gain.

A-MEN.

4 Give me joy or sadness,
  This be all my care,
That eternal gladness
  I with Thee may share.

5 Day by day prepare me
  As Thou seest best;
Then let angels bear me
  To Thy promised rest.
    AMEN.

SUPPLICATION FOR GUIDANCE.

O Jesus, I have promised.—*Concluded.*

4 O Jesus, Thou hast promised
　To all who follow Thee,
That where Thou art in glory
　There shall Thy servant be;
And, Jesus, I have promised
　To serve Thee to the end;
O give me grace to follow,
　My Master and my Friend.

5 O let me see Thy foot-marks,
　And in them plant mine own;
My hope to follow duly
　Is in Thy strength alone.
O guide me, call me, draw me,
　Uphold me to the end;
And then in heaven receive me,
　My Saviour and my Friend.

Thy way, not mine, O Lord. 144

H. BONAR, 1856.　　　　　　　　　　　　　　　J. R. FAIRLAMB, 1886.

1. Thy way, not mine, O Lord, How-ev-er dark it be!
　Lead me by Thine own hand;
　Choose out my path for me.
2. I dare not choose my lot: I would not, if I might;
　Choose Thou for me, my God,
　So shall I walk aright.
3. The kingdom that I seek Is Thine: so let the way
　That leads to it be Thine,
　Else I must surely stray.

4 Take Thou my cup, and it
　With joy or sorrow fill,
　As best to Thee may seem;
　Choose Thou my good and ill.

5 Not mine, not mine the choice,
　In things or great or small;
　Be Thou my Guide, my Strength,
　My Wisdom and my All.

Copyright, 1887, by The Century Co.

SUPPLICATION FOR GUIDANCE.

145. Gracious Saviour, gentle Shepherd.

JANE E. LEESON and J. WHITTEMORE.   J. R. FAIRLAMB, 1886.

1. Gra-cious Saviour, gen-tle Shep-herd, Lit-tle ones are dear to Thee;
2. Ten-der Shepherd, nev-er leave us From Thy fold to go a-stray;

Gathered with Thine arms, and car - ried   In Thy bo-som may we be;
By Thy look of love di-rect - ed,   May we walk the nar-row way;

Sweetly, fond-ly, safe-ly tend - ed,   From all want and dan-ger free.
Thus di-rect us, and pro-tect us,   Lest we fall an ea-sy prey.

3 Let Thy holy Word instruct us;
  Guide us daily by its light;
Let Thy love and grace constrain us
  To approve whate'er is right,
Take Thine easy yoke, and wear it,
  Strengthened with Thy heavenly might.

4 Taught to lisp the holy praises
  Which on earth Thy children sing,
Both with lips and hearts unfeigned
  May we our thank-off'rings bring;
Then with all the saints in glory
  Join to praise our Lord and King.

Copyright, 1887, by The Century Co.

SUPPLICATION FOR GUIDANCE. 146

Saviour, like a shepherd lead us.

3 Thou hast promis'd to receive us,
   Poor and sinful though we be;
   Thou hast mercy to relieve us;
   Grace to cleanse, and power to free.
   ||: Blessed Jesus, :||
   Let us early turn to Thee.

4 Early let us seek Thy favor,
   Early let us do Thy will;
   Holy Lord, our only Saviour!
   With Thy grace our bosoms fill
   ||: Blessed Jesus, :||
   Thou hast lov'd us, love us still. AMEN.

147 SUPPLICATION FOR GUIDANCE.

Jesus Christ our Saviour.

W. WHITING.　　　　　　　　　　　　　　　　　　　　N. H. ALLEN, 1886.

Allegretto.

1. Je-sus Christ our Sav-iour, Once for us a child, In Thy whole be-hav-ior Meek, o-be-dient, mild: In Thy footsteps tread-ing We Thy flock would be, Foe nor dan-ger dread-ing, While we fol-low Thee.

2. For all Thou be-stow-est, All Thou dost with-hold; What-so-e'er Thou know-est Best for us, Thy fold; For all gifts and gra-ces While we live be-low, Till in heav'nly plac-es We Thy face shall know. A-MEN.

3 We, Thy children, raising
　Unto Thee our hearts,
In Thy constant praising
　Bear our humble parts.
As Thy love hath won us
　From the world away,
Still Thy hands put on us;
　Bless us day by day.

4 Let Thine angels guide us,
　Let Thine arms enfold;
In Thy bosom hide us,
　Shelter'd from the cold;
To Thyself us gather,
　With the ransom'd host,
Praising Thee, the Father,
　And the Holy Ghost.　AMEN.

Copyright, 1887, by The Century Co.

SUPPLICATION FOR GUIDANCE.

My Saviour, be Thou near me.   148

A. T. Stowell   "Alpha."   J. H. Leslie.

1. My Saviour, be Thou near me When I lie down to sleep, And safe from ev-ery dan-ger My soul and bo-dy keep. With Thee there is no dark-ness, The light it shin-eth still; My Sav-iour, be Thou near me, And I shall fear no ill.
2. My Saviour, be Thou near me, When Sa-tan doth as - sail, To strengthen and pro-tect me, That he may not pre-vail. When sor-rows come up-on me, And days are dark and sad, My Sav-iour, be Thou near me, And I shall still be glad. A-men.

3 My Saviour, be Thou near me,
  In sickness and in pain,
To teach my spirit patience,
  To make my suff'ring gain;
When heart and flesh are failing,
  Receive my parting breath;
My Saviour, be Thou near me
  To comfort me in death.

4 And then, for ever near Thee,
  Safe in that happy place
Where angels sing Thy praises,
  And saints behold Thy face,
My joy shall be Thy presence,
  Yes, this my heav'n shall be,—
My Saviour shall be near me
  Through all eternity. Amen.

SUPPLICATION FOR GUIDANCE.

149. Father of love, our Guide and Friend.

W.J. Irons, 1853.   "St. Agnes."   J. B. Dykes, 1858.

1. Father of love, our Guide and Friend, O lead us gently on,
Until life's trial-time shall end, And heav'nly peace be won.
2. We know not what the path may be, As yet by us untrod,
But we can trust our all to Thee, Our Father and our God.
3. But if some darker lot be good, O teach us to endure
The sorrow, pain, or solitude, That makes the spirit pure. A-MEN.

4 Christ by no flow'ry pathway came,
And we, His servants here,
Must do Thy will and praise Thy name
In hope and love and fear.

5 And till in heav'n we sinless bow,
And faultless anthems raise,
O Father, Son and Spirit, now
Accept our feeble praise. AMEN.

---

150. O holy Saviour, Friend unseen.

Miss C. Elliott, 1834.   "Kirkstall."   F. Carr.

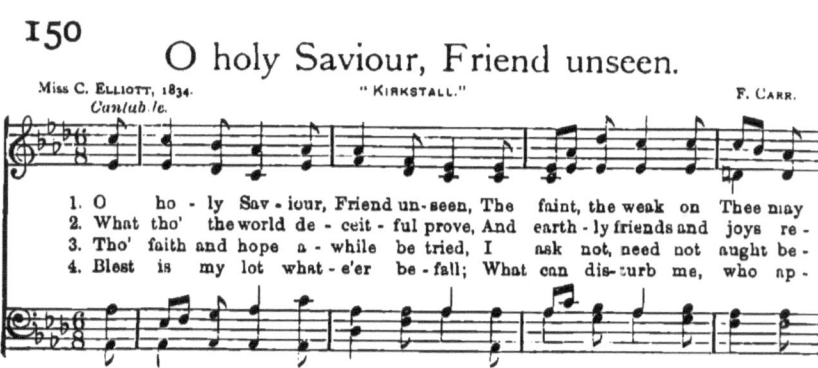

1. O holy Saviour, Friend unseen, The faint, the weak on Thee may
2. What tho' the world deceitful prove, And earthly friends and joys re-
3. Tho' faith and hope awhile be tried, I ask not, need not aught be-
4. Blest is my lot what-e'er be-fall; What can disturb me, who ap-

SUPPLICATION FOR GUIDANCE.

Lord, it belongs not to my care.

151

R. BAXTER, 1681. J. B. CALKIN.

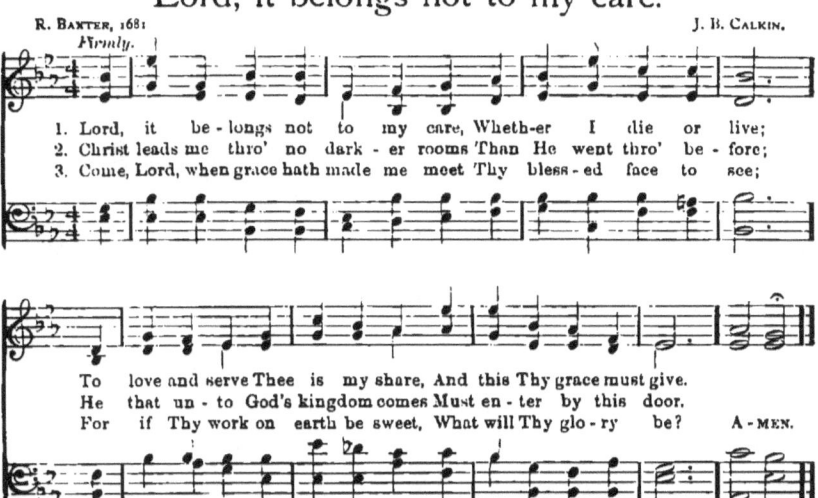

1. Lord, it be-longs not to my care, Wheth-er I die or live;
2. Christ leads me thro' no dark-er rooms Than He went thro' be-fore;
3. Come, Lord, when grace hath made me meet Thy bless-ed face to see;

To love and serve Thee is my share, And this Thy grace must give.
He that un-to God's kingdom comes Must en-ter by this door.
For if Thy work on earth be sweet, What will Thy glo-ry be? A-MEN.

4 There shall I end my sad complaints,
 My weary, sinful days,
And join with the triumphant saints
 That sing Jehovah's praise.

5 My knowledge of that life is small,
 The eye of faith is dim:
It is enough that Christ knows all,
 And I shall be with Him. AMEN.

O holy Saviour, Friend unseen.—*Concluded.*

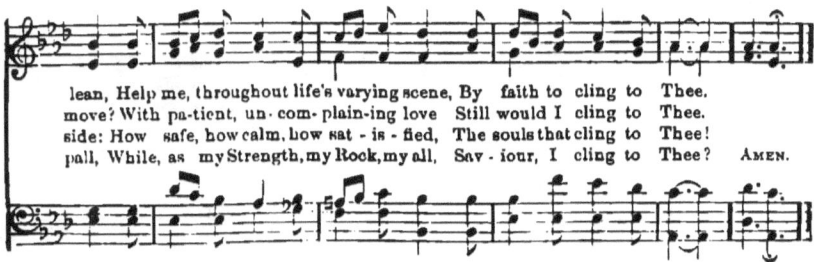

lean, Help me, throughout life's varying scene, By faith to cling to Thee.
move? With pa-tient, un-com-plain-ing love Still would I cling to Thee.
side: How safe, how calm, how sat-is-fied, The souls that cling to Thee!
pall, While, as my Strength, my Rock, my all, Sav-iour, I cling to Thee? AMEN.

152   **Thou art gone up on high.**   SUPPLICATION FOR GUIDANCE

Mrs. E. L. Toke, 1851.   J. Naylor, 1872.

1. Thou art gone up on high   To man-sions in the skies; And round Thy throne un-ceas-ing-ly The songs of praise a-rise. But we are ling'-ring here, With sin and care op-press'd; Lord, send Thy prom-is'd Com-fort-er, And lead us to Thy rest.

2. Thou art gone up on high; But Thou didst first come down Thro' earth's most bit-ter mis-er-y To pass un-to Thy crown; And girt with griefs and fears Our on-ward course must be; But on-ly let that path of tears Lead us at last to Thee!

3. Thou art gone up on high; But Thou shalt come a-gain, With all the bright ones of the sky At-tend-ant in Thy train. Lord, by Thy sav-ing power, So make us live and die, That we may stand in that dread hour At Thy right hand on high. A-MEN.

SUPPLICATION AT MORN AND EVE.

155. The morning bright, with rosy light.

T. O. SUMMERS, 1846.   "MORNING HYMN."   Mrs. E. A. B. CURTEIS, 1866.

Allegretto.

1. The morning bright, With ro-sy light, Has wak'd me from my sleep; Fa-
2. All thro' the day, I hum-bly pray, Be Thou my Guard and Guide; My
3. O make Thy rest With-in my breast, Great Spir-it of all grace; Make

ther, I own Thy love a-lone Thy lit-tle one doth keep.
sins for-give, And let me live, Lord Je-sus, near Thy side.
me like Thee, Then shall I be Pre-par'd to see Thy face. A-MEN.

156. Jesus, tender Shepherd, hear me.

Mrs. M. L. DUNCAN, 1839.   "ST. SYLVESTER."   J. B. DYKES, 1861.

Slowly.

1. Je-sus, ten-der Shepherd, hear me, Bless Thy lit-tle lamb to-night;
2. Thro' this day Thy hand has led me, And I thank Thee for Thy care;
3. Let my sins be all for-giv-en, Bless the friends I love so well;

Thro' the darkness be Thou near me, Keep me safe till morning-light.
Thou hast warm'd me, cloth'd me, fed me, List-en to my evening pray'r.
Take me, when I die, to heav-en, Hap-py there with Thee to dwell. A-MEN.

10

157 **O Thou, the contrite sinner's Friend.** SUPPLICATION.

Miss C. Elliott. *Andante.* English.

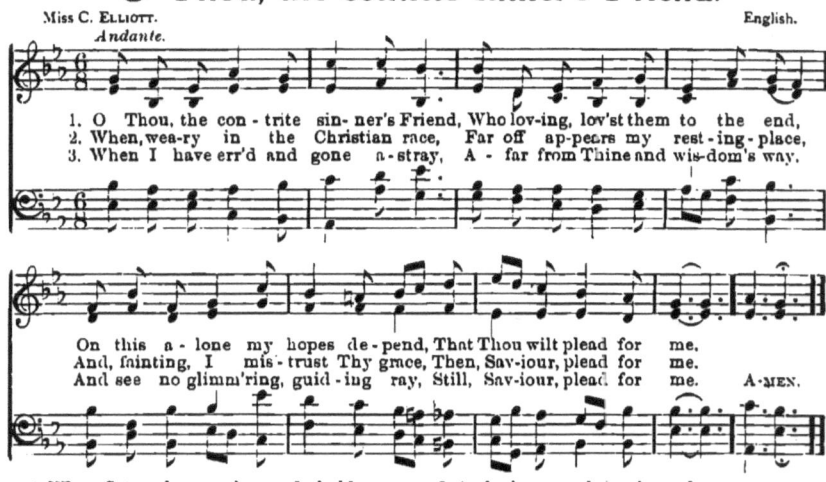

1. O Thou, the con-trite sin-ner's Friend, Who lov-ing, lov'st them to the end,
   On this a-lone my hopes de-pend, That Thou wilt plead for me.
2. When, wea-ry in the Christian race, Far off ap-pears my rest-ing-place,
   And, fainting, I mis-trust Thy grace, Then, Sav-iour, plead for me.
3. When I have err'd and gone a-stray, A-far from Thine and wis-dom's way,
   And see no glimm'ring, guid-ing ray, Still, Sav-iour, plead for me. A-MEN.

4 When Satan, by my sins made bold,
Strives from Thy cross to loose my hold,
Then with Thy pitying arms enfold,
And plead, O plead for me!

5 And when my dying hour draws near,
Darken'd with anguish, guilt, and fear,
Then to my fainting sight appear,
Pleading in heav'n for me. AMEN.

158 **Responses.**
[To Prayers, or to the Benediction.] W. S. P., 1887.

A — MEN. (or) A — MEN. (or) A — MEN.

[To Psalms, to the Beatitudes, or with Offerings, etc.]
Last time. Gregorian, adapted.

AL-LE-LU-IA! A-MEN. AL-LE-LU-IA! A-MEN.

Copyright, 1887, by The Century Co.

Songs of Trust and Consecration.

I lift my heart to Thee. 159

1. I lift my heart to Thee, Saviour Divine; For Thou art all to me, And I am Thine. Is there on earth a closer bond than this: That "my Beloved's mine, and I am His?"
2. Thine am I by all ties; But chiefly Thine, That thro' Thy sacrifice Thou, Lord, art mine. By Thine own cords of love, so sweetly wound Around me, I to Thee am closely bound.
3. I pray Thee, Saviour, keep Me in Thy love, Until death's holy sleep Shall me remove To that fair realm where, sin and sorrow o'er, Thou and Thine own are One for evermore. A-MEN.

160 Nearer, my God, to Thee.

TRUST.

Mrs. S. F. Adams, 1841.   "Mistley."   L. G. Hayne

Cantabile.

1. Near-er, my God, to Thee, Near-er to Thee! E'en though it be a cross That rais-eth me, Still all my song shall be— Near-er, my God, to Thee, Near-er to Thee.
2. Tho' like the wan-der-er, The sun gone down, Dark-ness be o-ver me— My rest a stone; Yet in my dreams I'd be Near-er, my God, to Thee, Near-er to Thee.
3. There let the way ap-pear Steps un-to heav'n, All that Thou send-est me In mer-cy giv'n; An-gels to beck-on me Near-er, my God, to Thee, Near-er to Thee. A-MEN.

4 Then, with my waking thoughts
   Bright with Thy praise,
Out of my stony griefs
   Bethel I'll raise;
So by my woes to be
Nearer, my God, to Thee,
   Nearer to Thee.

5 Or if on joyful wing
   Cleaving the sky,
Sun, moon, and stars forgot,
   Upward I fly,
Still all my song shall be,
Nearer, my God, to Thee,
   Nearer to Thee. AMEN.

My faith looks up to Thee. 161

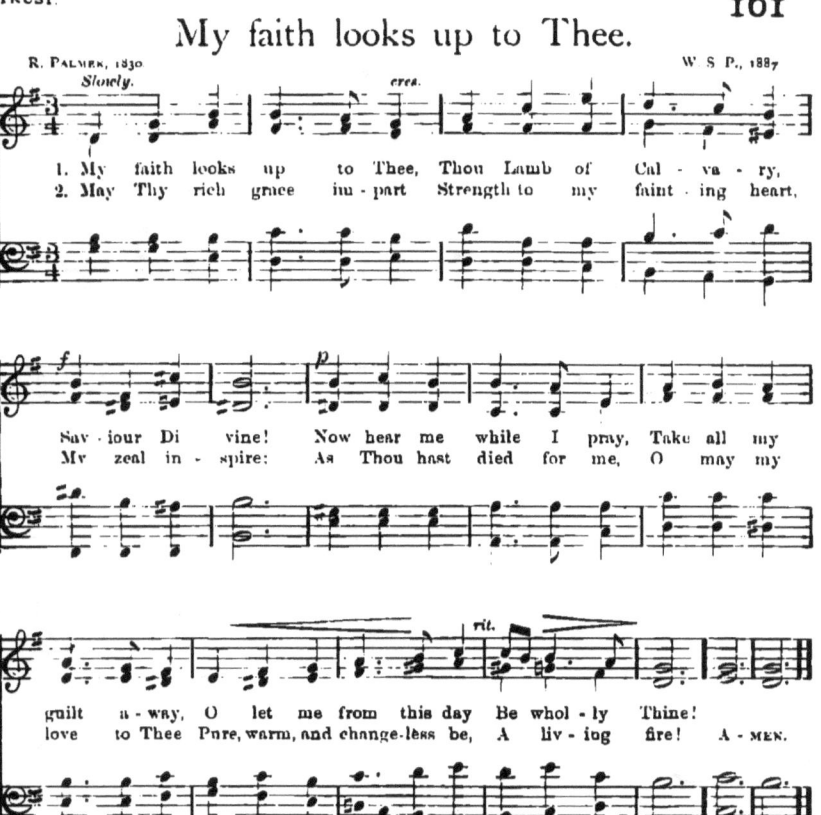

3 While life's dark maze I tread,
  And griefs around me spread,
    Be Thou my Guide;
  Bid darkness turn to day,
  Wipe sorrow's tears away,
  Nor let me ever stray
    From Thee aside.

4 When ends life's transient dream,
  When death's cold, sullen stream
    Shall o'er me roll,
  Blest Saviour, then in love
  Fear and distrust remove;
  O bear me safe above,
    A ransom'd soul! AMEN.

Copyright, 1887, by The Century Co.

162. Jesus, Lover of my soul.

TRUST.

C. WESLEY, 1740. "HOLLINGSIDE.." J. B. DYKES, 1861.

Andante.

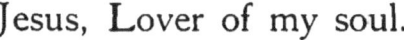

1. Je - sus, Lov - er of my soul, Let me to Thy bo - som fly,
While the wa - ters near - er roll, While the tem - pest still is high.
Hide me, O my Sav - iour, hide, Till the storm of life be past;
Safe in - to the ha - ven guide, O re - ceive my soul at last.

2. Oth - er ref - uge have I none, Hangs my help - less soul on Thee;
Leave, ah! leave me not a - lone, Still sup - port and com - fort me.
All my trust on Thee is stay'd, All my help from Thee I bring;
Cov - er my de - fence-less head With the shad - ow of Thy wing.

3. Plenteous grace with Thee is found, Grace to cov - er all my sin;
Let Thy heal - ing streams a - bound, Make and keep me pure with - in.
Thou of life the foun-tain art, Free - ly let me take of Thee;
Spring Thou up with-in my heart, Rise to all e - ter - ni - ty. A - MEN.

164. We saw Thee not when Thou didst tread.

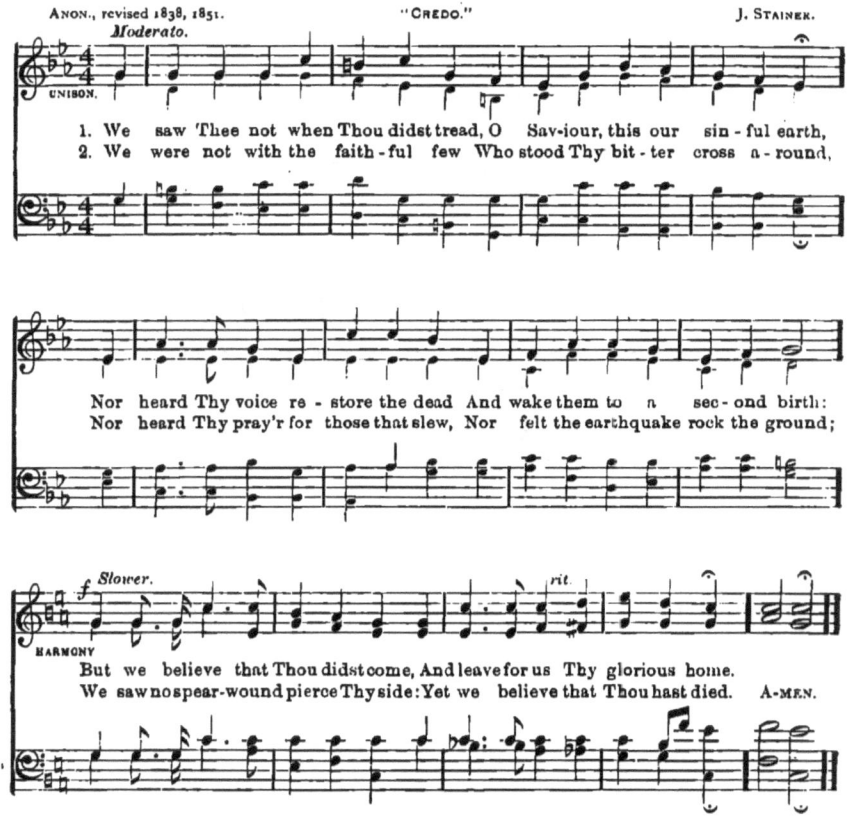

1. We saw Thee not when Thou didst tread, O Saviour, this our sinful earth,
Nor heard Thy voice restore the dead And wake them to a second birth:
But we believe that Thou didst come, And leave for us Thy glorious home.

2. We were not with the faithful few Who stood Thy bitter cross around,
Nor heard Thy pray'r for those that slew, Nor felt the earthquake rock the ground;
We saw no spear-wound pierce Thy side: Yet we believe that Thou hast died. A-MEN.

3 No angel's message met our ear
On that first glorious Easter-day:
"The Lord is ris'n, He is not here;
Come, see the place where Jesus lay!"
But we believe that Thou didst quell
The banded pow'rs of death and hell.

4 And now that Thou dost reign on high,
And still, our longing sight to bless,
No ray of glory from the sky
Shines down upon our wilderness:
Yet we believe that Thou art there,
And seek Thee, Lord, in praise and pray'r.
AMEN.

TRUST.

O Love Divine, that stooped to share. 165

O. W. HOLMES, 1848.   "ST. RAPHAEL."   E. SEYMOUR, 1873.
Cantabile.

1. O Love Divine, that stoop'd to share
   Our sharpest pang, our bitt'rest tear,
   On Thee we cast each earth-born care,
   We smile at pain while Thou art near.

2. Tho' long the weary way we tread,
   And sorrow crown each ling'ring year,
   No path we shun, no darkness dread,
   Our hearts still whisp'ring, Thou art near. A-MEN.

3 When drooping pleasure turns to grief,
   And trembling faith is changed to fear,
The murm'ring wind, the quiv'ring leaf,
   Shall softly tell us, Thou art near.

4 On Thee we fling our burd'ning woe,
   O Love Divine, for ever dear!
Content to suffer while we know,
   Living or dying, Thou art near! AMEN.

TRUST.

Art thou weary, art thou languid. 167

Greek, 8th Century. "STEPHANOS." H. W. Baker, 1861.
Con moto. FIRST TUNE.

1. Art thou wea-ry, art thou lan-guid, Art thou sore dis-trest?
2. Hath He marks to lead me to Him, If He be my Guide?
3. Is there di-a-dem, as mon-arch, That His brow a-dorns?

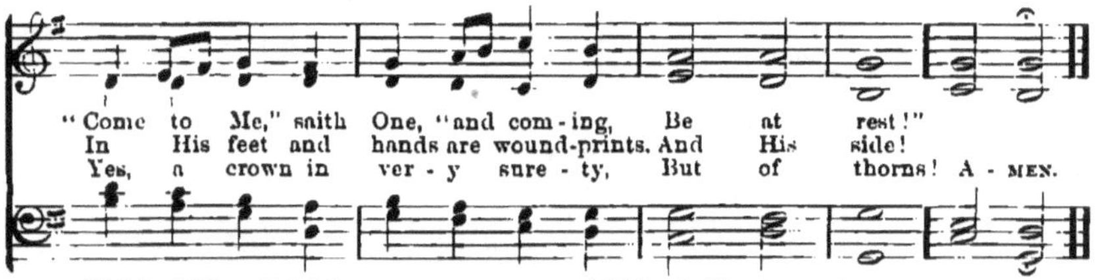

"Come to Me," saith One, "and com-ing, Be at rest!"
In His feet and hands are wound-prints. And His side!
Yes, a crown in ver-y sure-ty, But of thorns! A-MEN.

4 If I find Him, if I follow,
  What my portion here?
Many a sorrow, many a labor,
  Many a tear!
5 If I still hold closely to Him,
  What hath He at last?
Sorrow vanquish'd, labor ended,
  Jordan past!

6 If I ask Him to receive me,
  Will He say me nay?
Not till earth, and not till heaven
  Pass away!
7 Finding, following, keeping, struggling,
  Is He sure to bless?
Angels, martyrs, prophets, virgins,
  Answer, "Yes!" AMEN.

167a

Andante. SECOND TUNE. W. S. P., 1887.

TREBLES ONLY, OR A FEW VOICES

f

ALL

Copyright, 1887, by The Century Co.

168. I am trusting Thee, Lord Jesus.

TRUST.

Miss F. R. Havergal. — E. P. Parker.

1. I am trust-ing Thee, Lord Je-sus, Trust-ing on-ly Thee,
2. I am trust-ing Thee for par-don; At Thy feet I bow;
3. I am trust-ing Thee, Lord Je-sus, Nev-er let me fall;

Trust-ing Thee for full sal-va-tion Great and free.
For Thy grace and ten-der mer-cy, Trust-ing now.
I am trust-ing Thee for ev-er, And for all. A-men.

169. O cease, my wandering soul.

W. A. Muhlenberg, 1826. — "Dawn." — E. P. Parker.

Cantabile.

1. O cease, my wand'ring soul, On rest-less wing to roam; All this wide
2. Be-hold the ark of God! Be-hold the o-pen door! O haste to
3. There safe thou shalt a-bide, There sweet shall be thy rest, And ev-ery

world, to ci-ther pole, Hath not for thee a home.
gain that dear a-bode, And rove, my soul, no more.
long-ing sat-is-fied, With full sal-va-tion blest. A-men.

TRUST
Come, let us all unite and sing. 170

H. KINGSBURY.   S. P. WARREN, 1886.

1. Come, let us all u-nite and sing, "God is love." Let heav'n and earth their praises bring: God is love; Let ev-ery soul from sin awake, Each in his heart sweet mu-sic make, And sweet-ly sing for Je-sus' sake, "God is love."
2. O tell to earth's re-motest bound "God is love!" In Christ is full re-demp-tion found: God is love, His blood can cleanse our sins a-way; His Spir-it turns our night to day, And leads our soul with joy to say, "God is love." A-MEN.

3 What though our heart and flesh should fail:
   God is love,
Through Christ we shall o'er death prevail:
   God is love.
In Jordan's swell we need not fear,
For Jesus will be with us there
Our souls above the waves to bear:
   God is love.

4 In heaven we shall sing again,
   "God is love,"
Yes, this shall be our noblest strain,
   "God is love."
While endless ages roll along,
In concert with the heav'nly throng,
This still shall be our sweetest song.
   "God is love." AMEN.

Copyright, 1887, by The Century Co.

TRUST.

There's a Friend for little children.—Concluded.

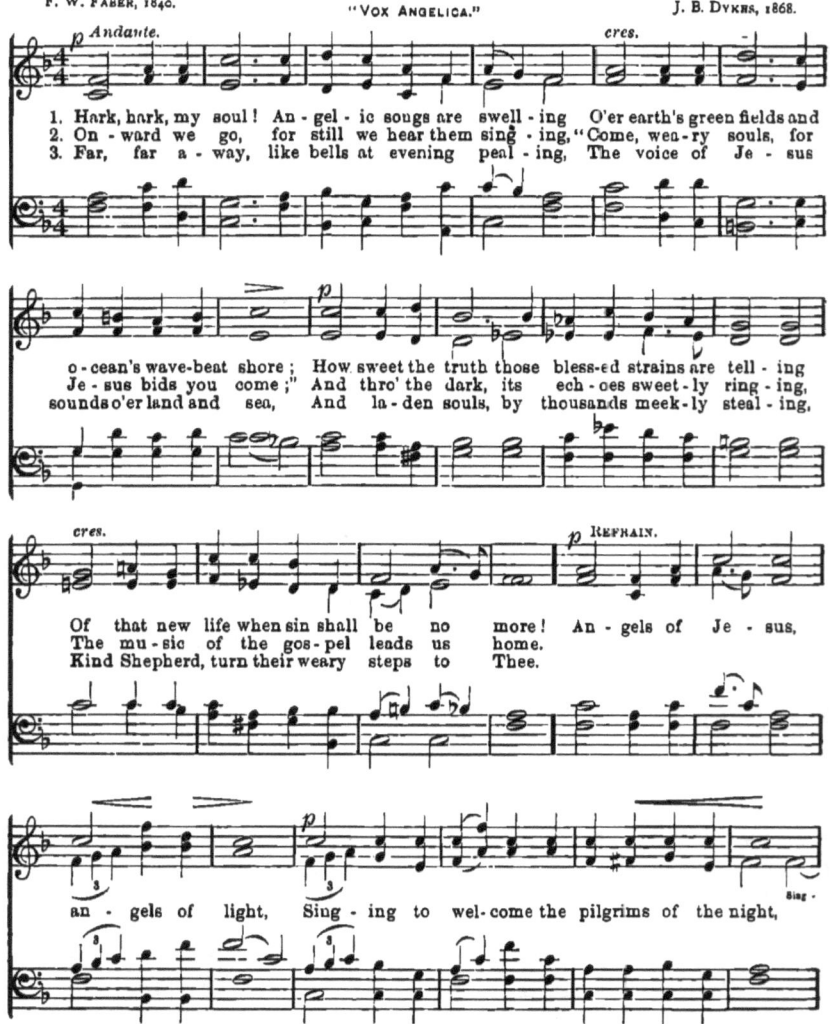

CONSECRATION.

Hark, hark, my soul!—*Concluded.*

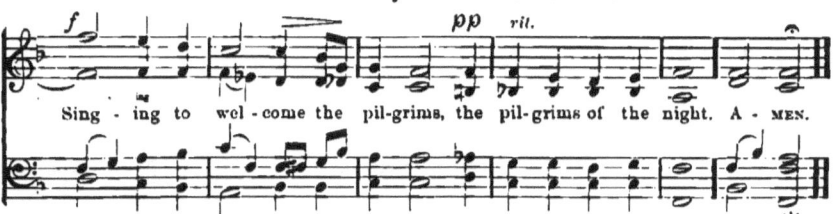

Sing-ing to wel-come the pil-grims, the pil-grims of the night. A-MEN.

4 Rest comes at length ; though life be long and dreary,
 The day must dawn and darksome night be past,
 Faith's journey ends in welcome to the weary,
 And heaven, the heart's true home, will come at last.—REF.

5 Angels, sing on, your faithful watches keeping,
 Sing us sweet fragments of the songs above ;
 Till morning's joy shall end the night of weeping,
 And life's long shadows break in cloudless love !—REF.

Through good report and evil, Lord. 177

H. BONAR. A. E. FISHER, 1886.

1. Thro' good re-port and e-vil, Lord, Still guid-ed by Thy faith-ful word,—
2. Strengthen'd by Thee we for-ward go, 'Mid smile or scoff of friend or foe,
3. O Mas-ter, point Thou out the way, Nor suf-fer Thou our steps to stray :

Our staff, our buck-ler, and our sword,—We fol-low Thee.
Thro' pain or ease, through joy or woe, We fol-low Thee.
Then in that path that leads to day We fol-low Thee. A-MEN.

4 Thou hast passed on before our face ;
 Thy footsteps on the way we trace ;
 Oh, keep us, aid us by Thy grace :
   We follow Thee.

5 Whom have we in the heaven above,
 Whom on this earth, save Thee, to love?
 Still in Thy light we onward move ;
   We follow Thee ! AMEN.

Copyright, 1897, by The Century Co.

CONSECRATION.

178 God of my life, Thy boundless grace.

Miss C. Elliott, 1841.   "ALMSGIVING."   J. B. Dykes.

1. God of my life, Thy bound-less grace Chose, pardon'd, and a-dopt-ed me; My Rest, my Home, my Dwell-ing-place, I come to Thee.
2. Je-sus, my Hope, my Rock, my Shield, Whose precious blood was shed for me, In-to Thy hands my soul I yield; I come to Thee. A-MEN.

3 Spirit of glory and of God,
   Long hast Thou deign'd my Guide to be;
   Now be Thy comfort sweet bestow'd;
   I come to Thee.

4 I come to join that countless host,
   Who praise Thy name unceasingly;
   Blest Father, Son, and Holy Ghost,
   I come to Thee. AMEN.

179 The Lord is my Shepherd.

Psalm 23.   F. Walker.

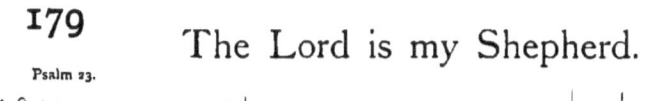

1 The Lord is my Shepherd; | I • shall not | want. ‖ He maketh me to lie down in green pastures; He leadeth me be- | side the | still | waters;

3 Yea, though I walk through the valley of the | shadow of | death, ‖ I will fear no evil; for | Thou art | with | me;

5 Thou hast anointed my | head with | oil; ‖ my | cup | runneth | over.

7 Glory be to the Father, | and • to the | Son, ‖ And | to the | Holy | Ghost;

CONSECRATION.

Just as I am. 180

Miss C. Elliott, 1836.   "St. Crispin."   G. J. Elvey.

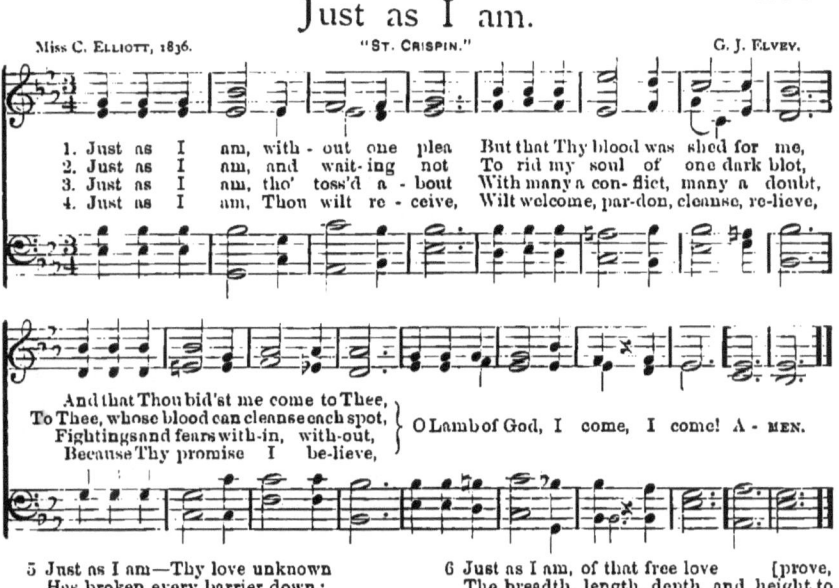

1. Just as I am, with-out one plea   But that Thy blood was shed for me,
2. Just as I am, and wait-ing not   To rid my soul of one dark blot,
3. Just as I am, tho' toss'd a-bout   With many a con-flict, many a doubt,
4. Just as I am, Thou wilt re-ceive,   Wilt welcome, par-don, cleanse, re-lieve,

And that Thou bid'st me come to Thee,
To Thee, whose blood can cleanse each spot,
Fightings and fears with-in, with-out,
Because Thy promise I be-lieve,
} O Lamb of God, I come, I come! A-MEN.

5 Just as I am—Thy love unknown
Has broken every barrier down;
Now, to be Thine, yea, Thine alone,
O Lamb of God, I come!

6 Just as I am, of that free love [prove,
The breadth, length, depth, and height to
Here for a season, then above,
O Lamb of God, I come! AMEN.

The Lord is my Shepherd.—*Concluded.*

2 He re- | storeth my | soul: ‖ He guideth me in the paths of righteousness | for His | name's | sake.
4 Thy rod and Thy staff, they | comfort | me. ‖ Thou preparest a table before me in the | pres- ence | of mine | enemies;
6 Surely goodness and mercy shall follow me all the | days • of my | life; ‖ And I will dwell in the | house • of the | Lord for | ever.
8 As it was in the beginning, is now, and | ever | shall be, ‖ World | without | end: A- | MEN.

CONSECRATION.

Jesus, Shepherd of the sheep.—*Concluded.*

CONSECRATION.

184. My blessed Saviour, is Thy love.

J. STENNETT, 1697. W. S. P., 1887.

1. My blessed Saviour, is Thy love So great, so full, so free? Behold, I give my love, my heart, My life, my all to Thee.
2. I love Thee for that glorious worth In Thy great self I see; I love Thee for that shameful cross Thou hast endur'd for me. A-MEN.

3 No man of greater love can boast
   Than for his friend to die;
   But for Thy foes, Lord, Thou wast slain:
   What love with Thine can vie?

4 Make us like Thee in meekness, love,
   In every beauteous grace,
   From glory thus to glory changed
   As we behold Thy face. AMEN.

Copyright, 1887, by The Century Co.

185. Jesus calls us o'er the tumult.

Mrs. C. F. ALEXANDER, 1853. "ST. MABYN." A. H. BROWN.

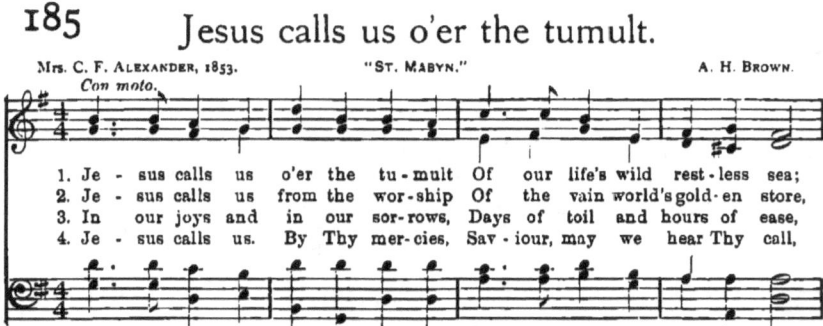

1. Jesus calls us o'er the tumult Of our life's wild restless sea;
2. Jesus calls us from the worship Of the vain world's golden store,
3. In our joys and in our sorrows, Days of toil and hours of ease,
4. Jesus calls us. By Thy mercies, Saviour, may we hear Thy call,

CONSECRATION.

Still, still with Thee, my God. 186

J. D. BURNS, 1856.   "ALDERSGATE."   G. P. MERRICK.

1. Still, still with Thee, my God, I would de-sire to be; By day, by night, at home, a-broad, I would be still with Thee.
2. With Thee, when dawn comes in, And calls me back to care; Each day re-turn-ing, to be-gin With Thee, my God, in pray'r.
3. With Thee, a-mid the crowd That throngs the bu-sy mart, To hear Thy voice, 'mid clam-or loud, Speak soft-ly to my heart. A-MEN.

4 With Thee, when day is done,
And evening calms the mind;
The setting, as the rising sun,
With Thee my heart would find.

5 With Thee, in Thee, by faith
Abiding I would be;
By day, by night, in life, in death,
I would be still with Thee. AMEN.

Jesus calls us o'er the tumult.—*Concluded.*

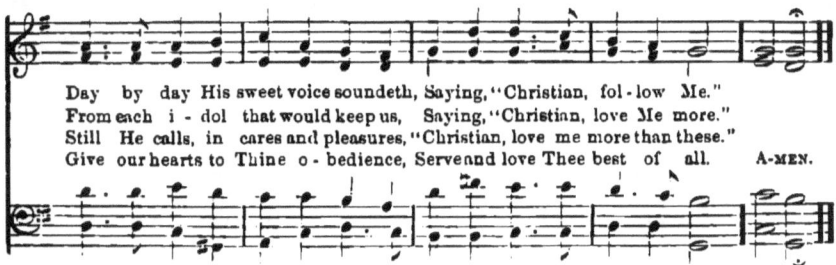

Day by day His sweet voice soundeth, Saying, "Christian, fol-low Me."
From each i-dol that would keep us, Saying, "Christian, love Me more."
Still He calls, in cares and pleasures, "Christian, love me more than these."
Give our hearts to Thine o-bedience, Serve and love Thee best of all. A-MEN.

CONSECRATION.

187. Now I have found a Friend.

H. J. McC. Hope, 1852.
Brightly.

G. A. Burdett, 1886.

1. Now I have found a Friend, Je-sus is mine; His love shall nev-er end, Je-sus is mine; Tho' earth-ly joys de-crease, Tho' earth-ly friendships cease, Now I have last-ing peace, Je-sus is mine.
2. Tho' I grow poor and old, Je-sus is mine; Tho' I grow faint and cold, Je-sus is mine; He shall my wants sup-ply, His pre-cious blood is nigh, Nought can my hope de-stroy, Je-sus is mine. A-MEN.

3 When earth shall pass away,
    Jesus is mine;
In the great judgment-day,
    Jesus is mine;
O what a glorious thing
Then to behold my King,
With tuneful voice to sing
    "Jesus is mine!"

4 Father, Thy name I bless,
    Jesus is mine;
Thine was the sov'reign grace,
    Praise shall be Thine.
Spirit of holiness,
Sealing the Father's grace,
By Thee I would embrace
    Jesus, as mine. AMEN.

Copyright, 1887, by The Century Co.

Songs of Work and Warfare.

Jesus, still lead on.

WARFARE.

Onward, Christian soldiers!—*Concluded.*

With the cross of Je - sus Go - ing on be - fore! A - MEN.

3 Crowns and thrones may perish,
  Kingdoms rise and wane,
  But the Church of Jesus
  Constant will remain:
  Gates of hell can never
  'Gainst that Church prevail;
  We have Christ's own promise,
  And that cannot fail.—REF.

4 Onward then, ye people,
  Join our happy throng,
  Blend with ours your voices
  In the triumph-song:
  Glory, praise, and honor
  Unto Christ the King;
  This through countless ages
  Men and angels sing.—REF. AMEN.

Uplift the banner!

190

G. W. DOANE, 1848.
Animato.
J. B. CALKIN, 1872.

1. Up - lift the ban - ner! Let it float Sky-ward and sea-ward, high and wide; The
2. Up - lift the ban - ner! An-gels bend In anx - ious si - lence o'er the sign, And
3. Up - lift the ban - ner! Wide and high, Sea-ward and sky-ward let it shine! Nor

sun shall light its shin-ing folds, The cross on which the Sav-iour died.
vain - ly try to com - prehend The won-der of the love di-vine.
skill nor might nor mer - it ours,—We con-quer on - ly in that sign. A - MEN.

WARFARE.

The Son of God goes forth to war. 192

R. HEBER, 1827.   "ELLACOMBE."   German.
Allegro.

1. The Son of God goes forth to war, A king-ly crown to gain;
2. The mar-tyr first, whose en-gle eye Could pierce be-yond the grave;

His blood-red ban-ner streams a-far:— Who fol-lows in His train?
D.S. Who pa-tient bears his cross be-low,— He fol-lows in His train.
   Who saw his Mas-ter in the sky, And called on Him to save.
D.S. He pray'd for them that did the wrong:—Who fol-lows in His train?

Who best can drink his cup of woe, Tri-umphant o-ver pain;
Like Him with par-don on his tongue, In midst of mor-tal pain, A-MEN.

3 A glorious band, the chosen few,
   On whom the Spirit came;
  Twelve valiant saints, their hope they knew,
   And mock'd the cross and flame.
  They met the tyrant's brandish'd steel,
   The lion's gory mane;
  They bow'd their necks the death to feel:—
   Who follows in their train?

4 A noble army, men and boys,
   The matron and the maid,
  Around the Saviour's throne rejoice,
   In robes of light arrayed.
  They climb'd the steep ascent of heav'n
   Through peril, toil, and pain:
  O God, to us may grace be giv'n
   To follow in their train. AMEN.

WARFARE.

Brightly gleams our banner.—*Concluded.*

Wav - ing on Christ's sol - diers To their home on high! A - MEN.

4 All our days direct us,
   In the way we go;
   Crown us still victorious
   Over every foe;
   Bid Thine angels shield us
   When the storm-clouds low'r;
   Pardon Thou and save us
   In the last dread hour. REF.

5 Then with saints and angels
   May we join above,
   Off'ring pray'rs and praises
   At Thy throne of love.
   When the march is over,
   Then come rest and peace,
   Jesus in His beauty,
   Songs that never cease! REF. AMEN.

194
Soldiers of Christ, arise!

C. WESLEY, 1749.
With emphasis.
"DAY OF PRAISE."
C. H. STEGGALL.

1. Sol - diers of Christ, a - rise! And put your ar - mor on, Strong
2. Strong in the Lord of Hosts, And in His might - y pow'r; Who
3. Stand, then, in His great might, With all His strength en - dued; And
4. That, hav - ing all things done, And all your con - flicts past, Ye

in the strength which God sup-plies Thro' His e - ter - nal Son;
in the strength of Je - sus trusts Is more than con - quer - or.
take, to arm you for the fight, The sword and shield of God:—
may o'er-come thro' Christ a - lone, And per - fect stand at last. A-MEN.

WARFARE.

A mighty fortress is our God.

"EIN' FESTE BURG."

3 And though this world, with devils fill'd,
   Should threaten to undo us,
  We will not fear, for God hath will'd
   His truth to triumph through us.
    The prince of darkness grim,
    We tremble not for him;
    His rage we can endure,
    For lo! his doom is sure,—
    One little word shall fell him.

4 That Word above all earthly pow'rs,
   In spite of them abideth;
  The spirit and the gifts are ours
   Through Him who with us sideth.
    Let goods and kindred go,
    This mortal life also;
    The body they may kill,—
    God's truth abideth still,
    His kingdom is for ever. AMEN.

WARFARE

199 Awake, my soul, stretch every nerve.

P. DODDRIDGE. 1740.   "CHRISTMAS."   G. F. HÄNDEL, 1728.

3 'Tis God's all-animating voice
   That calls thee from on high;
   'Tis His own hand presents the prize
   To thine aspiring eye.

4 Blest Saviour! introduced by Thee,
   Have I my race begun;
   And, crown'd with vict'ry, at Thy feet,
   I'll lay my honors down. AMEN.

201 On our way rejoicing.

WARFARE.

J. S. B. Monsell, 1863.
G. A. Burdett, 1886.

Animato.

1. On our way re - joic - ing, Home - ward as we move, Heark - en to our prais - es, O Thou God of love! Is there grief or sad - ness, Firm our trust shall be; Is our sky be - cloud - ed, Light shall come from Thee,
2. Je - sus Christ hath tri - umph'd, Van - quish'd is our foe; On our way re - joic - ing Glad - ly let us go! Christ with - out— our safe - ty; Christ with - in — our joy; Who, if we be faith - ful, Can our hope de - stroy?
3. Un - to God the Fa - ther Joy - ful songs we sing: Un - to God the Sav - iour Thank - ful hearts we bring; Un - to God the Spir - it Bow we and a - dore, On our way re - joic - ing, Now and ev - er - more.

Copyright, 1887, by The Century Co.

WARFARE.

Happy are we. 202

Mrs HERRICK JOHNSON.
B. C. BLODGETT, 1886.

Animato.

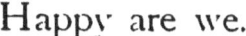

1. Hap - py are we,..... God's own lit - tle flock, Shel - tered so
2. What shall we do for the Mas - ter so dear? Oh, there are
3. Ma - ny He has who are not of this fold, Out in the

close in the cleft of the Rock, Far a - bove tem - pest, or
ma - ny in need of our cheer, Souls that know noth - ing but
storm and the pit - i - less cold; These we will win by our

dan - ger, or shock, Hap - py are we in.... Je - sus.
dark - ness and fear, Souls in the dark with - out Je - sus.
pray'rs and our gold, Win them to love our... Je - sus.

4 Over the mountains and over the seas,
Lovingly, joyfully, speed we to these,
Seeking to save them by tenderest pleas,
Save by the blood of Jesus.

5 Joyfully, then, let us spread the glad news,
Never this service for Jesus refuse,
Never a moment to work for Him lose;
Joyfully work for Jesus.

Copyright, 1887, by The Century Co.

WARFARE.

203 Hail to the brightness.

T. HASTINGS, 1830.   "LEILA."   M. COSTA.
Allegro.

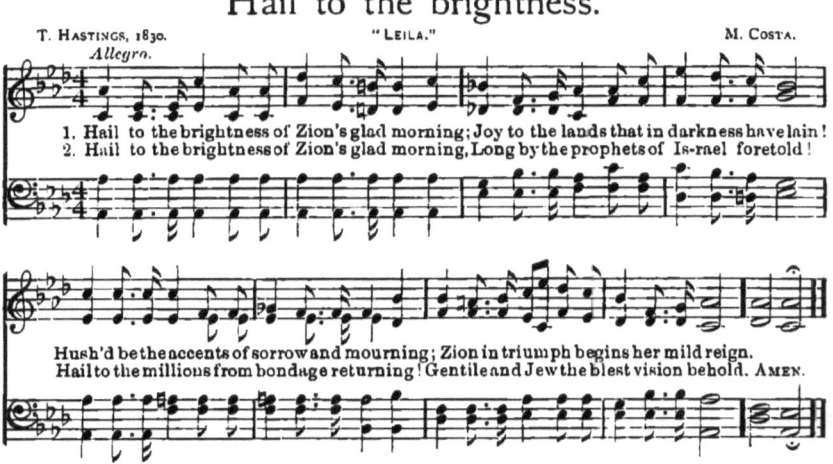

1. Hail to the brightness of Zion's glad morning; Joy to the lands that in darkness have lain!
2. Hail to the brightness of Zion's glad morning, Long by the prophets of Israel foretold!

Hush'd be the accents of sorrow and mourning; Zion in triumph begins her mild reign.
Hail to the millions from bondage returning! Gentile and Jew the blest vision behold. AMEN.

    3 Lo, in the desert rich flowers are springing;
      Streams ever copious are gliding along;
      Loud from the mountain-tops echoes are ringing;
      Wastes rise in verdure and mingle in song!

    4 See, from all lands, from the isles of the ocean,
      Praise to Jehovah ascending on high!
      Fall'n are the engines of war and commotion;
      Shouts of salvation are rending the sky. AMEN.

---

204 O Spirit of the living God.

J. MONTGOMERY, 1823.   "ALSTONE."   C. E. WILLING.
Con moto.

1. O Spirit of the living God, In all the fulness of Thy grace,
2. Give tongues of fire and hearts of love, To preach the reconciling Word;
3. Be darkness, at Thy coming, light; Confusion, order in Thy path;
4. Baptize the nations far and nigh, The triumphs of the Cross record;

WARFARE

Eternal Father, Thou hast said. 205

R. PALMER, 1830.   B. TOURS.
Maestoso.

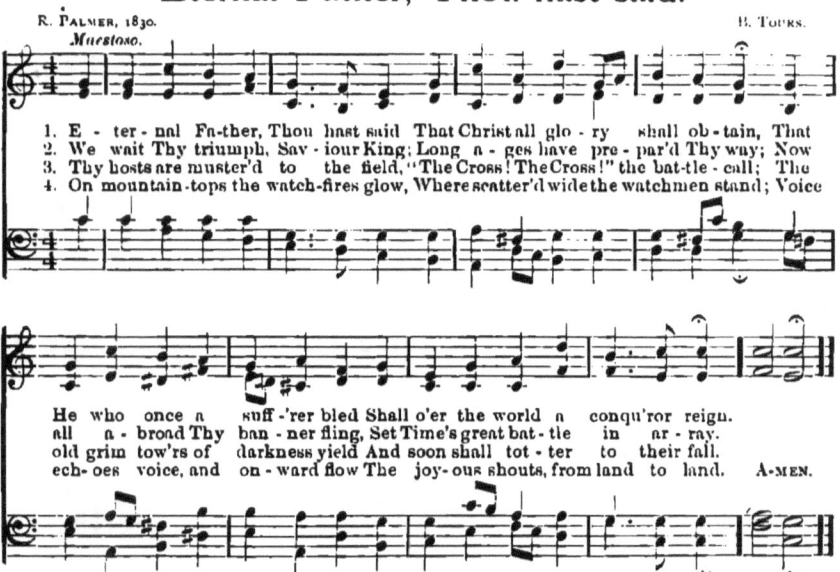

1. E-ter-nal Fa-ther, Thou hast said That Christ all glo-ry shall ob-tain, That He who once a suff-'rer bled Shall o'er the world a conqu'ror reign.
2. We wait Thy triumph, Sav-iour King; Long a-ges have pre-par'd Thy way; Now all a-broad Thy ban-ner fling, Set Time's great bat-tle in ar-ray.
3. Thy hosts are muster'd to the field, "The Cross! The Cross!" the bat-tle-call; The old grim tow'rs of darkness yield And soon shall tot-ter to their fall.
4. On mountain-tops the watch-fires glow, Where scatter'd wide the watchmen stand; Voice ech-oes voice, and on-ward flow The joy-ous shouts, from land to land. A-MEN.

5 Oh, fill Thy Church with faith and pow'r;
Bid her long night of weeping cease;
To groaning nations haste the hour,
Of life and freedom, light and peace.

6 Come, Spirit, make Thy wonders known!
Fulfil the Father's high decree;
Then earth, the might of hell o'erthrown,
Shall keep her last great jubilee. AMEN.

O Spirit of the living God.—*Concluded.*

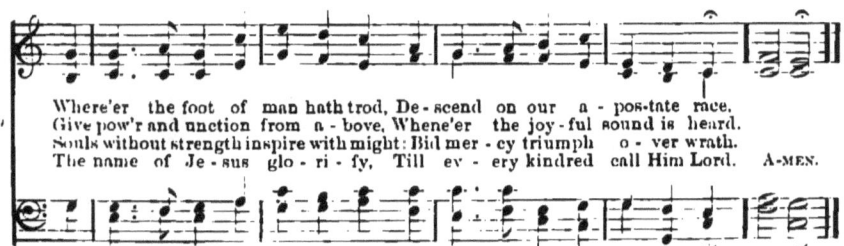

Where'er the foot of man hath trod, De-scend on our a-pos-tate race.
Give pow'r and unction from a-bove, Whene'er the joy-ful sound is heard.
Souls without strength inspire with might: Bid mer-cy triumph o-ver wrath.
The name of Je-sus glo-ri-fy, Till ev-ery kindred call Him Lord. A-MEN.

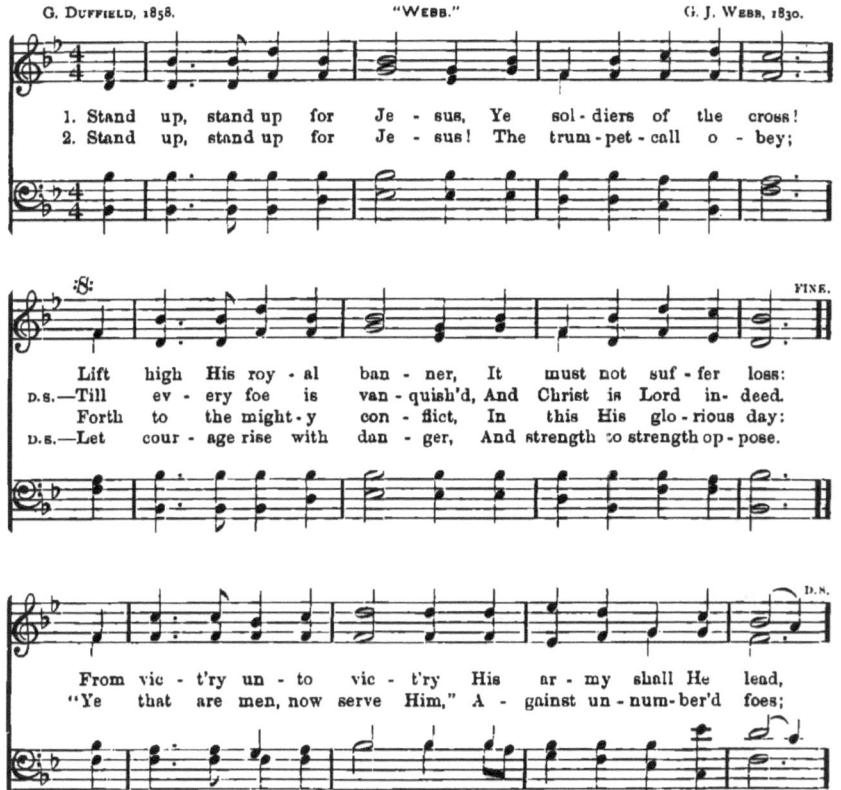

3 Stand up, stand up for Jesus!
   Stand in His strength alone;
   The arm of flesh will fail you—
   Ye dare not trust your own:
   Put on the Gospel-armor,
   Each piece put on with pray'r;
   Where duty calls, or danger,
   Be never wanting there.

4 Stand up, stand up for Jesus!
   The strife will not be long;
   This day, the noise of battle,
   The next, the victor's song;
   To him that over-cometh,
   A crown of life shall be:
   He with the King of glory
   Shall reign eternally.

WARFARE.

Christ for the world we sing! 207

S. Wolcott, 1869.   "Bermondsey."   Anon, 1781.
Con brio.

1. "Christ for the world" we sing; The world to Christ we bring, With lov-ing zeal; The poor, and them that mourn, The faint and o-ver-borne, Sin-sick and sor-row-worn, Whom Christ doth heal!
2. "Christ for the world" we sing; The world to Christ we bring, With fer-vent pray'r; The way-ward and the lost, By rest-less pas-sions toss'd, Redeem'd at count-less cost, From dark des-pair! A-men.

3 "Christ for the world" we sing;
  The world to Christ we bring,
    With one accord;
  With us the work to share,
  With us reproach to dare,
  With us the cross to bear,
    For Christ our God!

4 "Christ for the world" we sing;
  The world to Christ we bring,
    With joyful song;
  The new-born souls, whose days,
  Reclaim'd from error's ways,
  Inspir'd with hope and praise,
    To Christ belong! Amen.

SONGS OF HEAVEN.

Jerusalem on high.

209

210. Jerusalem the golden.

Latin, 12th Century. — "EWING." — A. Ewing, 1853.

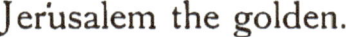

1. Je-ru-sa-lem the gold-en, With milk and hon-ey blest! Beneath thy con-tem-pla-tion Sink heart and voice oppress'd. I know not, O I know not What joys await us there, What ra-dian-cy of glo-ry, What light beyond com-pare!

2. They stand, those halls of Zi-on, All ju-bi-lant with song; And bright with many an an-gel And all the mar-tyr-throng. The Prince is ev-er in them, The day-light is se-rene; The pastures of the bless-ed Are deck'd in glorious sheen. A-MEN.

3 There is the throne of David,
And there, from care releas'd,
The shout of them that triumph,
The song of them that feast:
And they who, with their Leader
Have conquer'd in the fight,
For ever and for ever
Are clad in robes of white.

4 O sweet and blessed country,
The home of God's elect!
O sweet and blessed country
That eager hearts expect!
Jesus, in mercy bring us
To that dear land of rest,
Who art, with God the Father,
And Spirit, ever blest. AMEN.

HEAVEN.

Jerusalem, the glorious.

211

Latin, 12th Century.
Andante.

J. BARNBY.

1. Je - ru - sa - lem, the glor - ious, The glo - ry of th' e - lect,— O dear and fu - ture vis - ion That ea - ger hearts ex - pect! Ev'n now by faith I see thee, Ev'n here thy walls dis - cern; To thee my thoughts are kin - dled, And strive, and pant, and yearn!

2. The Cross is all thy splen - dor, The Cru - ci - fied, thy praise; His laud and ben - e - dic - tion Thy ran - som'd peo - ple raise;— Je - sus, the Crown of beau - ty, True God and Man they sing, Their nev - er - fail - ing Por - tion, Their glo - rious Lord and King.

3. O sweet and bless - ed coun - try! Shall I e'er see thy face? O sweet and bless - ed coun - try! Shall I e'er win thy grace? Je - ru - sa - lem! ex - ult - ing On that se - cur - est shore, I hope thee, wish thee, sing thee, And love thee ev - er - more. A-MEN.

HEAVEN.

"Forward!" be our watchword.—*Concluded.*

For-ward out of dark-ness, For-ward in-to light!
Till the veil be lift-ed, Till our faith be sight!
Pil-grims, to your coun-try For-ward in-to light!
For-ward in-to tri-umph, For-ward in-to light! A-MEN.

There is a happy land. 217

A. YOUNG, 1838. "HAPPY LAND." Hindoo melody.
Semplice.

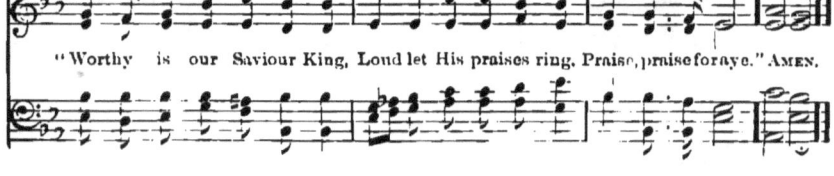

1. { There is a hap-py land, Far, far a-way,
   { Where saints in glo-ry stand, Bright, bright as day. } O how they sweetly sing,

"Worthy is our Saviour King, Loud let His praises ring. Praise, praise for aye." AMEN.

2 Come to this happy land,
  Come, come away;
 Why will ye doubting stand,
  Why still delay?
 O we shall happy be,
 When, from sin and sorrow free,
 Lord, we shall live with Thee,
  Blest, blest for aye.

3 Bright in that happy land
  Beams every eye;
 Kept by a Father's hand,
  Love cannot die.
 On, then, to glory run,
 Be a crown and kingdom won,
 And, bright above the sun,
  Reign, reign for aye. AMEN.

220 Sing Alleluia forth in duteous praise.

HEAVEN.

Latin, 5th Century.   "HOLY CITY."   A. SULLIVAN.

HEAVEN.

Sing Alleluia forth in duteous praise.—*Concluded.*

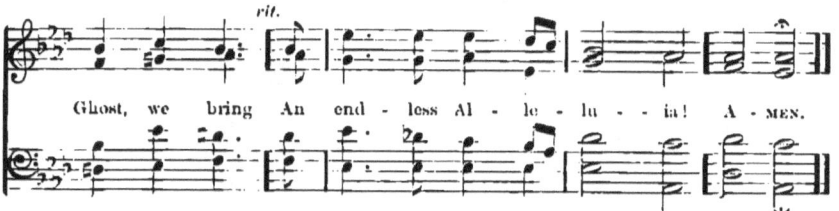

Who are these, like stars appearing. 221

German, 18th Century.   "ALL SAINTS."   German, about 1700.

1. Who are these, like stars appearing, These, before God's throne who stand?
   Each a golden crown is wearing—Who are all this glorious band?
   Alleluia! hark they sing, Praising loud their heav'nly King!

2. These are they who have contended For their Saviour's honor long,
   Wrestling on till life was ended, Foll'wing not the sinful throng;
   These, who well the fight sustain'd, Triumph thro' the Lamb have gain'd. A-MEN.

3 These are they whose hearts were riven,
   Sore with woe and anguish tried,
Who in pray'r full oft have striven
   With the God they glorified;
Now, their painful conflict o'er,
God has bid them weep no more.

4 These like priests have watched and waited,
   Off'ring up to Christ their will,
Soul and body consecrated,
   Day and night to serve Him still:
Now in God's most holy place
Blest they stand before His face. AMEN.

HEAVEN.

222 For all Thy saints

W. W. How, 1854. J. Barnby, 1868.

1. For all Thy saints, who from their la-bors rest, Who Thee by
   faith before the world con-fess'd, Thy Name, O Je-sus,
   be for ev-er blest!
2. Thou wast their Rock, their Fort-ress, and their Might; Thou, Lord, their
   Cap-tain in the well-fought fight; Thou in the dark-ness
   drear their one true Light.
3. O may Thy sold-iers, Faith-ful, true, and bold, Fight as the
   saints who no-bly fought of old. And win, with them, the
   victor's crown of gold.

Al-le-lu-ia! Al-le-lu-ia! A-men.

4 O blest communion! fellowship divine!
We feebly struggle; they in glory shine!
Yet all are one in Thee, for all are Thine! Alleluia!

5 And when the strife is fierce, the warfare long,
Steals on the ear the distant triumph-song,
And hearts are brave again, and arms are strong! Alleluia!

6 But lo! there breaks a yet more glorious day;
The saints triumphant rise in bright array;
The King of Glory passes on His way! Alleluia!

7 From earth's wide bounds, from ocean's farthest coast,
Through gates of pearl streams in the countless host,
Singing to Father, Son, and Holy Ghost—Alleluia! Amen.

4 O Paradise! O Paradise!
 We long to sin no more;
 We long to be as pure on earth
  As on thy spotless shore;
   Where loyal hearts, etc.

5 Lord Jesus, King of Paradise,
 Oh, keep us in Thy love,
 And guide us to that happy land
 Of perfect rest above:
  Where loyal hearts, etc. AMEN.

HEAVEN.

I'm but a stranger here. 225

T. R. TAYLOR, 1835. A. S. SULLIVAN, 1872.

1. I'm but a stranger here, Heav'n is my home; Earth's joys soon dis-ap-pear, Heav'n is my home. Dan-ger and sor-row stand Round me on ev-ery hand; Heav'n is my fa-ther-land, Heav'n is my home.
2. What tho' the tempest rage, Heav'n is my home; Short is my pil-grim-age, Heav'n is my home. For time's wild, wintry blast Soon will be o-ver-past; I shall reach home at last, Heav'n is my home. A-MEN.

3 There at my Saviour's side,
   Heav'n is my home;
I shall be glorified,
   Heav'n is my home.
There are the good and blest,
Those I love most and best;
And there I too shall rest,
   Heav'n is my home.

4 Therefore I murmur not,
   Heav'n is my home;
Whate'er my earthly lot,
   Heav'n is my home.
For I shall surely stand
There at my Lord's right hand;
Heav'n is my fatherland,
   Heav'n is my home! AMEN.

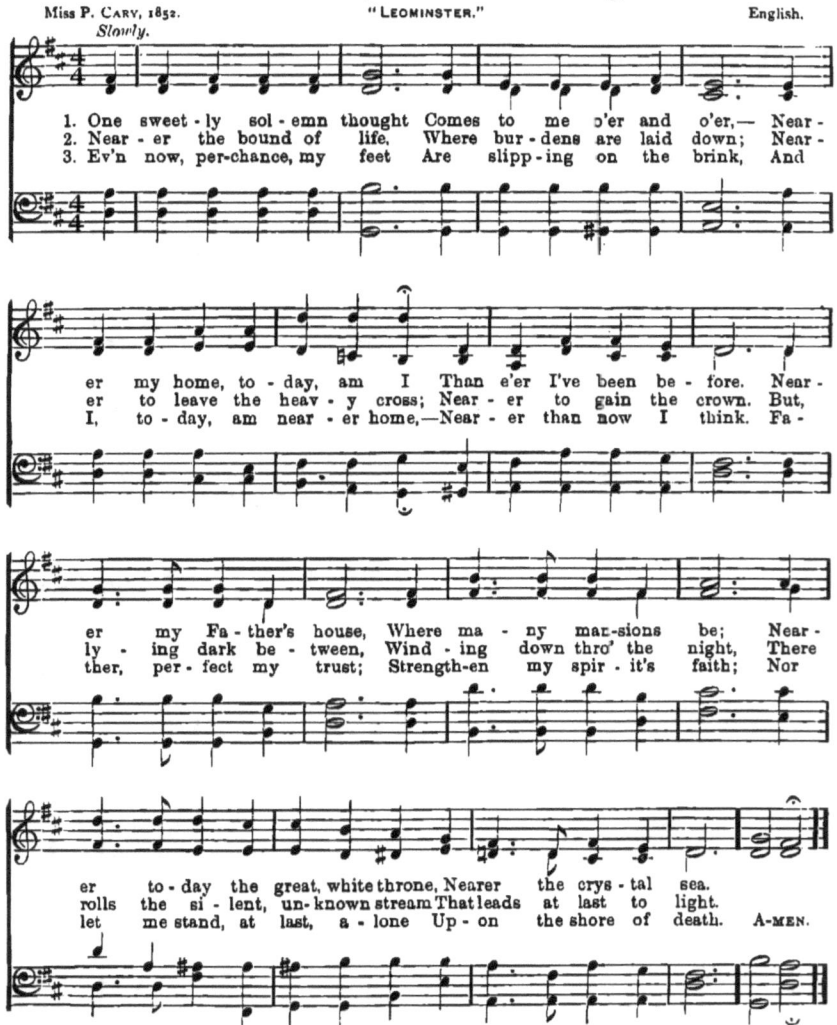

Songs for Special Days.

All my heart this night rejoices. 230

1. All my heart this night re-joi-ces, As I hear, Far and near,
2. Hark! a voice from yon-der man-ger, Soft and sweet, Doth en-treat—
3. Come, then, let us hast-en yon-der; Here let all, Great and small,
4. Thee, O Lord, with heed I'll cher-ish, Live to Thee, And with Thee

Sweet-est an-gel voi-ces. "Christ is born!" their choirs are sing-ing,
"Flee from woe and dan-ger; Breth-ren, come; from all that grieves you
Kneel in awe and won-der; Love Him who with love is yearn-ing;
Dy-ing, shall not per-ish; But shall dwell with Thee for ev-er,

Till the air Ev-ery-where Now with joy is ring-ing.
You are freed; All you need I will sure-ly give you."
Hail the Star, That from far Bright with hope is burn-ing.
Far on high, In the joy That can al-ter nev-er. A-MEN.

231. Hark! the herald angels sing.

CHRISTMAS.

C. WESLEY, 1739. "HERALD ANGELS." F. MENDELSSOHN, 1840.

1. Hark! the her-ald an-gels sing, "Glo-ry to the new-born King, Peace on earth, and mer-cy mild, God and sin-ners re-con-cil'd!" Joy-ful all ye na-tions, rise, Join the tri-umph of the skies! With th'angel-ic host proclaim, "Christ is born in Beth-le-hem."

2. Christ, by high-est heav'n a-dor'd; Christ, the ev-er-last-ing Lord! Late in time be-hold Him come, Off-spring of a vir-gin's womb! Veil'd in flesh the Godhead see; Hail th'in-carnate De-i-ty! Pleas'd as Man with men to dwell, Je-sus our Im-man-u-el!

3. Hail the heav'nly Prince of Peace! Hail the Sun of Righteousness! Light and life to all He brings, Ris'n with heal-ing in His wings. Mild He lays His glo-ry by, Born that man no more may die, Born to raise the sons of earth, Born to give them sec-ond birth.

Hark! the herald an-gels sing, "Glo-ry to the new-born King!" AMEN.

CHRISTMAS.

O'er Bethlehem's hill, in days of old.—*Concluded.*

3 So, gracious Spirit, by Thy light
  Shine Thou upon our way,
To guide our feet to Christ the Lord,
  Who would our homage pay;
For He who is the children's King
Will not disdain what children bring. Ref.

4 Not wise men we, with princely robes,
  With off'rings rich and rare,
We come with empty hands, O Lord,
  Burden'd with sin and care,
With hands that wrought Thy misery;—
And yet Thou bidd'st us come to Thee. Ref.

5 For gifts, we give ourselves to Thee;
  Our hearts shall be Thy throne;
For gold, we give Thee all our love;
  O make it all Thine own!
As incense sweet, Thy praise we sing,
And bless Thy name, our Saviour-King. Ref. Amen.

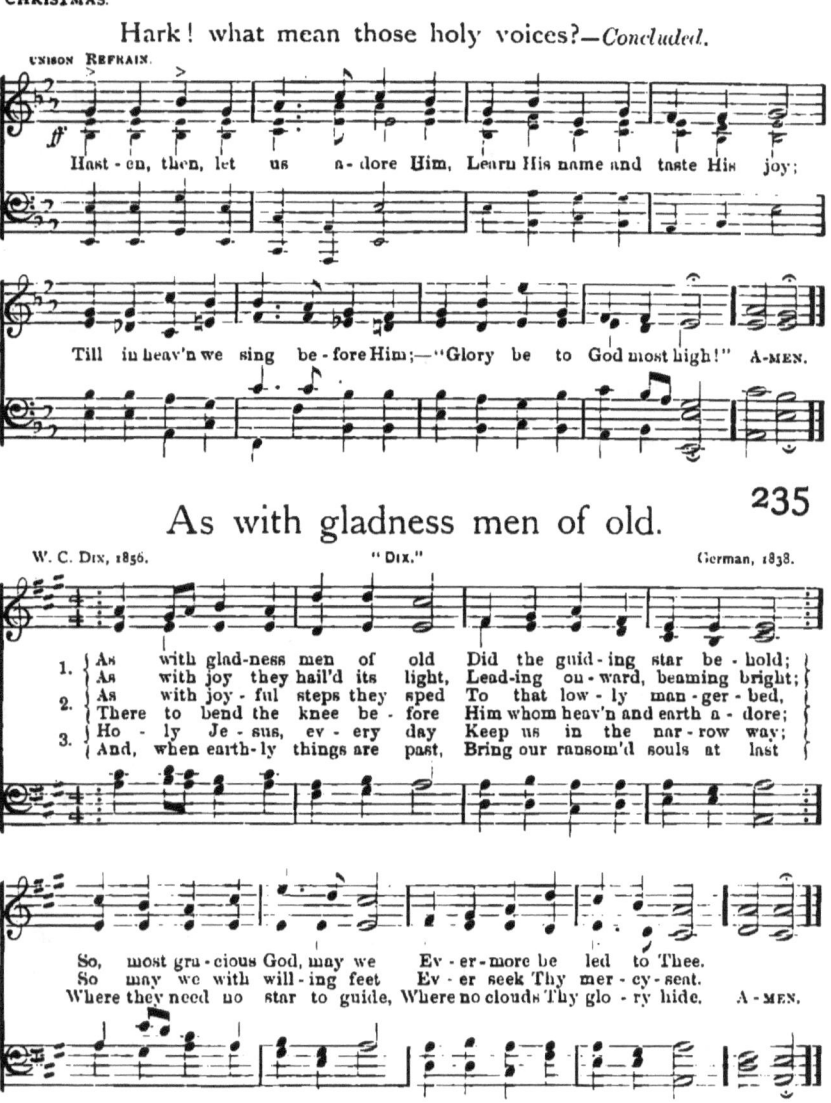

||: 3 Silent night! holiest night!
   Guiding star, O lend thy light! :||
   See the eastern wise men bring
   Gifts and homage to our King!
   Christ the Saviour is here!

||: 4 Silent night! holiest night!
   Wondrous Star, O lend thy light! :||
   With the angels let us sing
   Alleluia to our King!
   Christ our Saviour is here! AMEN.

CHRISTMAS

Joy fills our inmost heart.—*Concluded.*

sweet - er sound than this is heard,—Im - man - u - el! Im - man - u - el!

There came a little Child to earth. 239

Mrs. E. E. S. Elliott, 1873.   "CHRISTMAS."   R. N. Matthews.

Semplice.

1. There came a lit - tle Child to earth Long a - go; And
2. Out on the night, so calm and still Their song was heard; For they
3. And far a - way in a good - ly land, Fair and bright, Chil -
4. They sing how the Lord of that world so fair A child was born; And that

an - gels of God pro - claim'd His birth High and low.
knew the child on Bethl'hem's hill Was Christ the Lord.
dren with crowns of glo - ry stand, Rob'd in white.
they might crowns of glo - ry wear, Wore crown of thorn; A-MEN.

5 And in mortal weakness, in want and pain,
   Came forth to die,
That children of earth might ever reign
   With Him on high.

6 And ever more in their robes most fair
   And undefil'd
Those ransom'd children His praise declare,
   Who was once a Child. AMEN.

240 Once in royal David's city.

CHRISTMAS.

Mrs. C. F. Alexander, 1848. "Irby." H. J. Gauntlett, 1856.

1. Once in roy-al Da-vid's cit-y Stood a low-ly cat-tle-shed,
Where a moth-er laid her ba-by In a man-ger for His bed:
Ma-ry was the moth-er mild, Je-sus Christ her lit-tle child.

2. He came down to earth from heav-en Who is God and Lord of all,
And His shel-ter was a sta-ble, And His cra-dle was a stall;
With the poor, and mean, and lowly, Liv'd on earth our Sav-iour holy. A-MEN.

3 But our eyes at last shall see Him,
   Through His own redeeming love,
For that child so dear and gentle
   Is our Lord in heav'n above;
And He leads His children on
   To the place where He is gone.

4 Not in that poor lowly stable,
   With the oxen standing by,
We shall see Him; but in heaven,
   Set at God's right hand on high;
When like stars His children rise,
   Singing praises in the skies. AMEN.

CHRISTMAS.

Brightest and best. 241

R. HEBER, 1811.   "ST. NINIAN."   J. B. DYKES.

N. B.—The first stanza should be repeated at the close of the hymn.

1. Brightest and best of the sons of the morning, Dawn on our darkness and lend us thine aid; Star of the East, the horizon adorning, Guide where our infant Redeemer is laid.
2. Cold on His cradle the dew-drops are shining, Low lies His head with the beasts of the stall; Angels adore Him in slumber reclining, Maker and Monarch and Saviour of all. A-MEN.

3 Say, shall we yield Him, in costly devotion,
    Odors of Edom, and off'rings divine,
    Gems of the mountain, and pearls of the ocean,
    Myrrh from the forest, or gold from the mine?

4 Vainly we offer each ample oblation,
    Vainly with gifts would His favor secure;
    Richer by far is the heart's adoration,
    Dearer to God are the pray'rs of the poor. AMEN.

CHRISTMAS.

Good news on Christmas morning.—*Concluded.*

5. Thank God on Christmas morn - ing, Thank God, O chil - dren dear!
That Christ who came to Beth - le - hem, Is liv - ing now, and here.

Bright was the guiding star. 243

Miss H. AUBER, 1829.   "BANSTEAD."   ANON, 1886.

1. Bright was the guid - ing star that led, With mild, be - nig - nant ray, The wise men to the low - ly shed Where the Re - deem - er lay.
2. But lo! a bright - er, clear - er light Now points to His a - bode; It shines thro' sin and sor - row's night, To guide us to our God.
3. O glad - ly tread the nar - row path While light and grace are giv'n; Who meek - ly fol - low Christ on earth, Shall reign with Him in heav'n. A-MEN.

CHRISTMAS.

Hail to the Lord's Anointed!

245

J. MONTGOMERY, 1822.
A. E. FISHER, 1886.

Con moto.

1. Hail to the Lord's A-noint-ed, Great Da-vid's great-er Son!
2. He shall come down like show-ers Up-on the fruit-ful earth,
3. Kings shall fall down be-fore Him, And gold and in-cense bring:
4. O'er ev-ery foe vic-to-rious, He on His throne shall rest;

Hail, in the time ap-point-ed, His reign on earth be-gun!
And love and joy, like flow-ers, Spring in His path to birth:
All na-tions shall a-dore Him; His praise all peo-ple sing;
From age to age more glo-rious, All-bless-ing and all-blest.

He comes to break op-pres-sion, To set the cap-tive free,
Be-fore Him, on the mount-ains, Shall peace the her-ald go,
For He shall have do-min-ion O'er riv-er, sea, and shore,
The tide of time shall nev-er His co-ve-nant re-move;

To take a-way trans-gres-sion, And rule in e-qui-ty.
And right-eousness in fount-ains From hill to val-ley flow.
Far as the ea-gle's pin-ion Or dove's light wing can soar.
His name shall stand for ev-er; His great, best name of Love. A-MEN.

Copyright, 1887, by The Century Co.

CHRISTMAS

246 I think, when I read that sweet story of old.

Mrs. J. LUKE, 1841. J. H. CORNELL, 1871.

1. I think, when I read that sweet sto-ry of old, When Je-sus was here a-mong men, How He call'd lit-tle children as lambs to His fold, I should like to have been with them then.
2. I wish that His hands had been placed on my head, That His arm had been thrown a-round me, And that I might have seen His kind look when He said, "Let the lit-tle ones come un-to Me."
3. Yet still to His foot-stool in pray'r I may go, And ask for a share in His love; And if I thus earn-est-ly seek Him be-low, I shall see Him and hear Him a-bove— A-MEN.

By permission.

4 In that beautiful place He has gone to prepare
  For all who are wash'd and forgiv'n;
  And many dear children are gathering there,
  "For of such is the kingdom of heav'n."

5 But thousands and thousands who wander and fall,
  Never heard of that heavenly home;
  I should like them to know there is room for them all,
  And that Jesus has bid them to come. AMEN.

THE CRUCIFIXION.

O Thou, th' eternal Son of God. 249

W. C. Dix.   H. J. Gauntlett, 1872.
Solemnly.

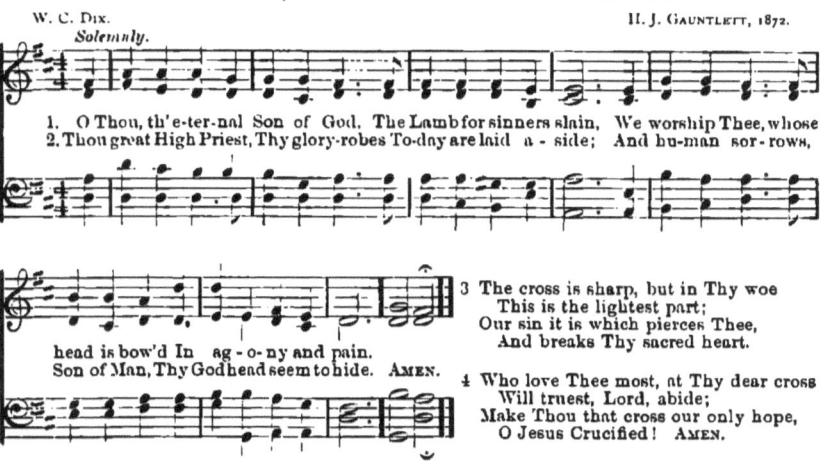

1. O Thou, th' e-ter-nal Son of God, The Lamb for sinners slain, We worship Thee, whose head is bow'd In ag-o-ny and pain.
2. Thou great High Priest, Thy glory-robes To-day are laid a - side; And hu-man sor - rows, Son of Man, Thy Godhead seem to hide. AMEN.

3 The cross is sharp, but in Thy woe
   This is the lightest part;
   Our sin it is which pierces Thee,
   And breaks Thy sacred heart.

4 Who love Thee most, at Thy dear cross
   Will truest, Lord, abide;
   Make Thou that cross our only hope,
   O Jesus Crucified! AMEN.

So rest, my Rest. 250

German, 1716.   "ARIMATHEA."   J. B. Calkin, 1872.
Slowly.

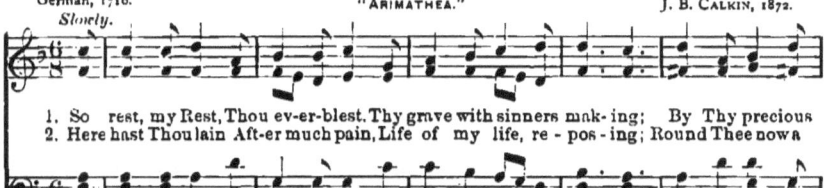

1. So rest, my Rest, Thou ev-er-blest, Thy grave with sinners mak- ing; By Thy precious death, from sin My dead soul a - wak- ing.
2. Here hast Thou lain Aft-er much pain, Life of my life, re - pos - ing; Round Thee now a rock-hewn grave, Rock of Ages, clos- ing. AMEN.

3 Breath of all breath,
   I know from death
  Thou wilt my dust awaken;
   Wherefore should I dread the grave,
  Or my faith be shaken?

4 Meantime I will,
   My Jesus, still
  Deep in remembrance lay Thee,
  Musing on Thy death; in death
  Be with me, I pray Thee. AMEN.

EASTER.

253. "Welcome, happy morning!"

Latin, 6th Century.
A. E. Fisher, 1886.

Brightly.

1. "Welcome, hap-py morn-ing!" Age to age shall say; Hell to-day is van-quish'd; Heav'n is won to-day. Lo! the Dead is liv-ing, God for ev-er-more! Him, their true Cre-a-tor, All His works a-dore.

2. Earth with joy con-fess-es, Cloth-ing her for Spring, All good gifts are com-ing With her ris-en King: Bloom in ev-ery mead-ow, Leaves on ev-ery bough, Speak His sor-rows end-ed, Hail His tri-umph now.

3. Months in due suc-ces-sion, Days of length'ning light, Hours and pass-ing mo-ments Praise Thee in their flight; Brightness of the morn-ing, Sky and fields and sea, Van-quish-er of dark-ness, Bring their praise to Thee.

REFRAIN.

"Welcome, hap-py morn-ing!" Age to age shall say;

Copyright, 1887, by The Century Co.

EASTER.

"Welcome, happy morning!"—Concluded.

4 Thou, of Life the Author,
Death didst undergo,
Tread the path of darkness,
Saving strength to show;
Come, then, True and Faithful,
Now fulfil Thy word;
'Tis the promis'd morning;
Rise, O buried Lord! REF.

5 Loose the souls long prison'd,
Bound with Satan's chain;
All that now is fallen,
Raise to life again;
Show Thy face in brightness,
Bid the nations see;
Bring again our daylight:
Day returns with Thee. REF.

254 Come, let us sing the song of songs.

J. MONTGOMERY, 1853.   "DUKE STREET."   J. HATTON, 1790.

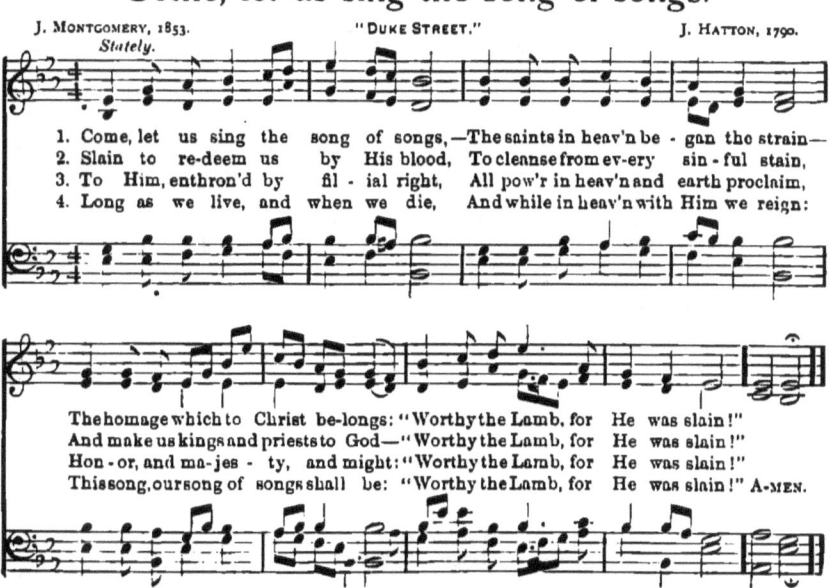

1. Come, let us sing the song of songs,—The saints in heav'n be-gan the strain—
2. Slain to re-deem us by His blood, To cleanse from ev-ery sin-ful stain;
3. To Him, enthron'd by fil-ial right, All pow'r in heav'n and earth proclaim,
4. Long as we live, and when we die, And while in heav'n with Him we reign:

The homage which to Christ be-longs: "Worthy the Lamb, for He was slain!"
And make us kings and priests to God—"Worthy the Lamb, for He was slain!"
Hon-or, and ma-jes-ty, and might: "Worthy the Lamb, for He was slain!"
This song, our song of songs shall be: "Worthy the Lamb, for He was slain!" A-MEN.

EASTER.

255 Jesus lives! Thy terrors now.

German, 18th Century.
J. R. FAIRLAMB, 1886.

1. Je - sus lives! Thy ter - rors now Can no long - er,
2. Je - sus lives! Hence-forth is death But the gate of
3. Je - sus lives! For us He died: Then, a - lone to

death, ap - pal us; Je - sus lives! By this we know
life im - mor - tal; This shall calm our trem - bling breath,
Je - sus liv - ing, Pure in heart may we a - bide,

Thou, O grave, canst not en - thral us. Al - le - lu - ia!
When we pass its gloom - y por - tal. Al - le - lu - ia!
Glo - ry to our Sav - iour giv - ing. Al - le - lu - ia! A-MEN.

Copyright, 1887, by The Century Co.

    4   Jesus lives! Our hearts know well
        Nought from us His love shall sever;
        Life, nor death, nor pow'rs of hell
        Tear us from His keeping ever. Alleluia!

    5   Jesus lives! To Him the throne
        Over all the world is given;
        May we go where He is gone,
        Rest and reign with Him in heav'n. Alleluia! AMEN.

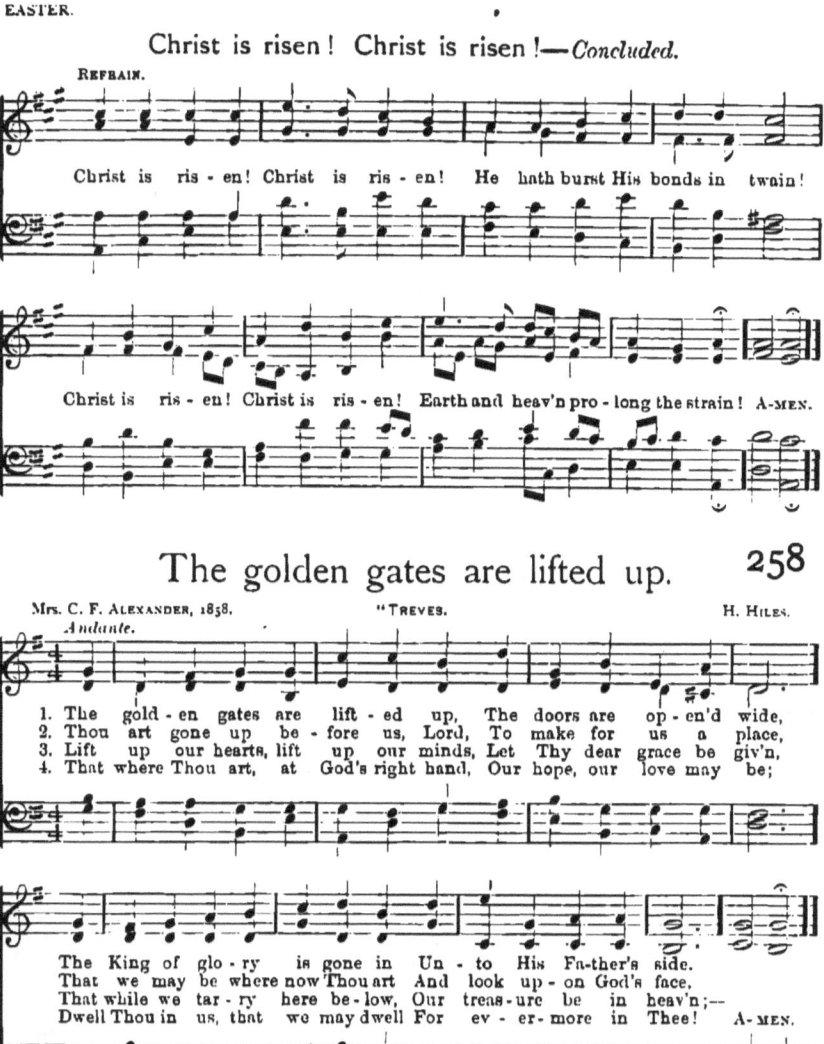

259 The strife is o'er, the battle done.

EASTER.

Latin. "CHRISTENDOM." J. W. Elliott.

Alleluia! Alleluia! Alleluia!
1. The strife is o'er, the battle done: The victory of life is won: The song of triumph has begun,—
2. He brake the mighty chains of hell; The bars from heav'n's high portals fell; Let hymns of praise His triumph tell,—
3. The pow'rs of death have done their worst, But Christ their legions hath dispers'd; Let shout of holy joy outburst,—

Alleluia!
4. Lord, by the stripes which wounded Thee, From death's dread sting Thy servants free, That we may live, and sing to Thee Alleluia. A-men.

ASCENSION.

Golden harps are sounding.—*Concluded.*

ASCENSION.

Our Lord is risen from the dead.

263

C. WESLEY, 1743.
Con moto.

J. BARNBY, 1872.

1. Our Lord is ris-en from the dead; Our Je-sus is gone up on high;
2. "Loose all your bars of mas-sy light, And wide un-fold th' e-the-real scene;
3. Lo! His tri-umph-al char-iot waits, And an-gels chant the sol-emn lay,—

The pow'rs of hell are cap-tive led, Dragg'd to the por-tals of the sky.
He claims these mansions as His right; Re-ceive the King of glo-ry in."
"Lift up your heads, ye heav'nly gates! Ye ev-er-last-ing doors, give way!"

There His tri-umph-al char-iot waits, And an-gels chant the sol-emn lay,—
"Who is the King of glory?—who?" "The Lord, that all our foes o'ercame,
"Who is the King of glory?—who?" "The Lord, of glo-rious pow'r possess'd;

"Lift up your heads, ye heav'nly gates! Ye ev-er-last-ing doors, give way!"
World, sin, and death, and hell o'erthrew; And Je-sus is the Conqueror's name."
The King of saints and an-gels too; God o-ver all, for ev-er blest." AMEN.

ASCENSION.

264. Hail the day that sees Him rise.

C. WESLEY, 1739.   "ASCENSION."   W. H. MONK.

1. Hail the day that sees Him rise— Alleluia!
   To His throne above the skies; Alleluia!
   Christ, awhile to mortals giv'n, Alleluia!
   Reascends His native heav'n. Alleluia!

2. There the glorious triumph waits; Alleluia!
   Lift your heads, eternal gates! Alleluia!
   Wide unfold the radiant scene; Alleluia!
   Take the King of glory in. Alleluia!

3. Him though highest heav'n receives, Alleluia!
   Still He loves the earth He leaves; Alleluia!
   Though returning to His throne, Alleluia!
   Still He calls mankind His own. Alleluia!

4. Lord, though parted from our sight, Alleluia!
   High above yon azure height, Alleluia!
   Grant our hearts may thither rise, Alleluia!
   Following Thee beyond the skies. Alleluia!

A-MEN.

INDEX OF AUTHORS.

[THE DATE OF THE BIRTH OF LIVING AUTHORS IS NOT GIVEN.]

Adams, *Mrs.* Sarah (Flower) [1805–1848] 160
Addison, Joseph [1672–1719] 99
Alexander, *Mrs.* Cecil Frances 160, 185, 228, 240, 258
Alford, *Dean* Henry, D. D. [1810–1871] 104, 216, 219
Auber, *Miss* Harriet [1773–1862] 33, 112, 243

Baker, *Sir* Henry Williams [1821–1877] 45, 89, 120
Bakewell, *Rev.* John [1721–1819]..85
Baring-Gould, *Rev.* Sabine ...16, 189
Barton, Bernard [1784–1849] 48
Baxter, *Rev.* Richard [1615–1689]..151
Bickersteth, *Bishop* Edw'd Henry, D. D. 67
Bode, *Rev.* John Ernest [1816–1874] 143
Bonar, *Rev.* Horatius, D. D. 12, 113, 144, 175, 177, 182
Bridges, Matthew 83
Browne, *Rev.* Simon [1680–1732]..113
Burns, *Rev.* James Drummond [1823–1864] 163, 186
Cary, *Miss* Phoebe [1825–1871] ... 229
Cawood, *Rev.* John [1775–1852] 47, 234
Cennick, *Rev.* John [1717–1755] 76
Chandler, *Rev.* John [1806–1876] ... 42
Chapman, *Miss* E. D. 260
Collins, *Rev.* Henry 133
Cooke, *Rev.* Henry, D. D. [1788–1868] 161
Cowper, William [1731–1800] 173
Coxe, *Bishop* Arthur Cleveland, D. D. 86
Cross, *Mrs.* Ada (Cambridge) 8
Crossman, *Rev.* Samuel [1624–1683] 209
Cummins, *Rev.* James John [d. 1867] 123

Deck, *Rev.* James George 78
Denny, *Sir* Edward 128
Dix, William Chatterton 77, 174, 235, 238, 249
Doane, *Bishop* George Washington, D. D. [1799–1859] 190
Doddridge, *Rev.* Philip, D. D. [1702–1751] 199
Dodge, *Mrs.* Mary Mapes 242
Doudney, *Miss* Sarah 95
Dracup, *Rev.* John [d. 1795] 52
Duffield, *Rev.* George 206
Duncan, *Mrs.* Mary (Lundie) [1814–1840] 156

Edmeston, James [1791–1867]..20, 153
Ellerton, *Rev.* John 7, 15, 21, 36, 51, 53
Elliott, *Miss* Charlotte [1789–1871] 40, 150, 157, 178, 180
Elliott, *Mrs.* Emily Elizabeth (Steele) 239

Faber, *Rev.* Frederic William, D. D. [1814–1863] 27, 62, 176, 224

Grant, *Sir* Robert [1785–1838] 70
Gurney, *Rev.* Archer Thompson [1802–1862] 257
Hammond, *Rev.* William [1719–1783] 226
Hart, *Rev.* Joseph [1712–1768] 107
Hastings, Thomas, Mus. Doc. [1784–1872] 203
Havergal, *Miss* Frances Ridley [1836–1879] 81, 168, 261
Heber, *Bishop* Reginald, D. D. [1783–1826] 22, 58, 192, 208, 241
Hodder, Edwin 50
Holmes, Oliver Wendell 61, 165
Hope, Henry Joy McCrackan [1809–1872] 187
How, *Bishop* William Walsham 1, 44, 101, 119, 125, 137, 222
Irons, *Rev.* William Josiah, D. D. [1812–1883] 149
Jervis, *Rev.* Thomas [1748–1833]... 38
Johnson, *Mrs.* Herrick 202
Keble, *Rev.* John [1792–1866] 19
Kelly, *Rev.* Thomas [1769–1855] 29, 56, 262
Kempthorne, *Rev.* John [1775–1838] 66
Ken, *Bishop* Thomas, D. D. [1637–1711] 28
Kennedy, *Rev.* Benjamin Hall 10
Key, Francis Scott [1799–1843] 94
King, *Rev.* John [1788–1858] 248
Kingsbury, H. 170
Lathbury, *Miss* Mary A 18
Leeson, *Miss* Jane Elizabeth 140, 145
Longfellow, *Rev.* Samuel 25, 108
Luke, *Mrs.* Jemima (Thompson) 246
Lynch, *Rev.* Thomas Toke [1818–1871] 110
Lyte, *Rev.* Henry Francis [1793–1847] 14, 31, 68, 84

Mant, *Bishop* Richard, D. D. [1776–1848] 98
Mason, *Rev.* John [d. 1694] 9
Maude, *Mrs.* Mary Fawler 227
Midlane, Albert 171
Monsell, *Rev.* John Samuel Bewley, LL.D. [1811–1875] 54, 97, 201
Montgomery, James [1771–1854] 35, 43, 59, 204, 244, 245, 254
Mudie, Charles Edward 159
Muhlenberg, *Rev.* William Augustus, D. D. [1796–1877] 169
Nelson, *Earl* Horatio 218
Newman, *Cardinal* John Henry, D. D. 142
Newton, *Rev.* John [1725–1807]..9, 198
Palgrave, Francis Turner ...127, 154
Palmer, *Rev.* Ray, D. D. [1808–1887] 132, 181, 205
Parker, *Rev.* Edwin Pond, D. D. 122, 126
Parson, *Mrs.* Elizabeth (Rooker)..2
Pearse, M. G. 233

Perronet, *Rev.* Edward [1726–1792] 74
Pierpoint, Folliott Sandford 100
Pollock, Thomas Benson ...109, 138, 141
Pott, *Rev.* Francis 41
Potter, *Rev.* Thomas Johnson [1827–1853] 193
Proctor, *Miss* Adelaide Anne [1825–1864] 23, 92
Rawson, George 2
Russell, *Rev.* Arthur Tozer [1806–1874] 17, 69, 80
Sears, *Rev.* Edmund Hamilton [1810–1876] 232
Steele, *Miss* Anne [1717–1778].46, 134
Stennett, *Rev.* Joseph, D. D. [1663–1713] 184
Stone, *Rev.* Samuel John 124, 127
Stowell, *Rev.* Thomas Alfred .. 148
Summers, Thomas Osmond 155
Taylor, *Rev.* Thomas Rawson [1807–1835] 225
Thring, *Rev.* Godfrey ..26, 64, 82, 130
Thrupp, *Miss* Dorothy Anne [1779–1847] 146
Toke, *Mrs.* Emma (Leslie) [1812–1878] 152
Toplady, *Rev.* Augustus Montague [1740–1778] 116
Tuttiett, *Rev.* Lawrence ...129, 247
Waring, *Miss* Anna Laetitia 172
Waring, *Samuel* Miller 55
Watts, *Rev.* Isaac, D. D. [1674–1748] 63
Wesley, *Rev.* Charles [1708–1788] 6, 37, 71, 121, 131, 136, 162, 191, 194, 231, 252, 263, 264
Whiting, William [1825–1878] 147
Whitmore, *Lady* Lucy E. G. [1792–1840] 30
Whittemore, *Rev.* Jonathan [1802–1860] 145
Williams, *Rev.* Isaac, D. D. [1802–1865] 135
Wolcott, *Rev.* Samuel, D. D. [1813–1886] 207
Woodford, *Bishop* James Russell, D. D. [1820–1855] 72
Wordsworth, *Bishop* Christopher, D. D. [1807–1885] ..4, 96, 223, 256, 265
Young, Andrew 217

From the Bible.34, 39, 49, 57, 73, 102, 103, 139, 158, 179, 248
Translated, from the Latin 60, 65, 75, 87, 88, 90, 91, 105, 106, 111, 114, 117, 118, 210, 211, 212, 213, 214, 220, 237, 253, 259
— From the Greek 167, 251
— From the German 11, 13, 32, 79, 93, 183, 188, 196, 221, 230, 238, 250, 255
— From the Danish 195
Anonymous 5, 164, 200, 215

INDEX OF COMPOSERS.

[THE DATE OF THE BIRTH OF LIVING COMPOSERS IS NOT GIVEN.]

Adcock, James [1778-1860]..........26
Allen, N. H.....................32, 147

Baker, *Sir* Henry Williams [1821-1877]........................167
Bambridge, W. S................195
Barnby, Joseph
    15, 16, 51, 97 (263), 107, 111, 133, 193, 211, 222, 224, 236
Bartlett, Homer N......110, 200, 238
Beethoven, Ludwig van [1770-1827]
    66
Black, J........................38
Blodgett, Benjamin Coleman, Mus. Doc.....................t.....63, 202
Booth, Josiah.....................209
Boyd, William...................129
Brown, Arthur Henry.........4, 185
Buck, Dudley......................78
Burdett, George A..9, 138, 187, 201, 234

Calkin, John Baptiste...151, 190, 250
Carr, F..........................150
Carter, *Rev.* Edmund S..........72
Chope, *Rev.* Richard Robert......45
Cooper, Joseph Thomas [1810-1880]
    90a
Cornell, John Henry
    136, 140, 246, 248, 261
Costa, *Sir* Michael.................203
Croft, William, Mus. Doc. [1677-1727]........................63, 70
Crotch, William, Mus. Doc. [1775-1847].......................59, 90a
Curtels, *Mrs.* Elizabeth Anna (Ball)
    155

Damrosch, Leopold, Mus. Doc. [1832-1885]....................260
Darwall, *Rev.* Leicester............188
Dickinson, *Rev.* Charles John....47
Dykes, *Rev.* John Bacchus, Mus. Doc. [1823-1876]
    58, 74, 89, 105, 112, 118, 130, 142a, 149, 156, 162, 174, 176, 178, 219, 226, 241

Elliott, James William ..64, 143, 259
Elvey, *Sir* George Job, Mus. Doc.
    83, 104, 180
Ewing, Alexander.................210

Fairlamb, J. Remington
    28, 137, 144, 145, 172, 255
Farrant, Richard [1530-1580].....139
Farrer, J. Downing...............121
Fisher, Arthur R.
    95, 132, 153, 177, 245, 253
Flood, E..........................59
Florio, Caryl............77, 80, 123, 262

Garrett, George Mursell, Mus. Doc.
    46, 227, 248

Gauntlett, Henry John, Mus. Doc. [1806-1876]........134 (249), 191, 240,
Gilbert, Walter Bond, Mus. Doc.
    31, 43
Gilchrist, W. W......12, 154, 182, 233
Goodwin, J........................50
Goss, *Sir* John, Mus. Doc. [1800-1880]...........................60
Gounod, Charles François.........55

Händel, Georg Friedrich [1685-1759]
    8, 34, 199
Harper, W. H....................42
Harrison, W....................113
Hatton, Frances J...............242
Hatton, John...................254
Haydn, Franz Josef [1732-1809]
    71, 198
Hayne, *Rev.* Leighton George, Mus. Doc..........................160
Henley, *Rev.* Phocion [1728-1764]..60
Hervey, *Rev.* Frederic Alfred John
    228
Hiles, Henry, Mus. Doc......23, 258
Hopkins, Edward John, Mus. Doc.
    22, 30, 98
Hopkins, John Larkin, Mus. Doc. [1820-1873]....................103
Hullah, John, LL.D. [1812-1884]..173
Hyde, Dorsey W................163

Jekyll, Charles Sherwood..........29

Langran, James, Mus. Doc......124
Lawes, Henry [1595-1662] 91a
Leslie, Henry David 6
Leslie, J. H....................148
Lomas, G 114

Macfarren, George Alexander, Mus. Doc....................1, 5, 91a, 247
Main, Hubert Platt..............109
Mallary, *Rev.* R. De Witt........25
Maker, F. C......................92
Mason, Lowell, Mus. Doc. [1792-1872]........................208
Matthews, H. N.................239
Matthews, *Rev.* Timothy Richard
    61
Mendelssohn-Bartholdy, Felix [1809-1847].................131, 231
Merrick, *Sir* G. P...............186
Monk, Edwin George, Mus. Doc. 33
Monk, William Henry.......14, 264
Mosenthal, Joseph..........13, 163
Mudie, Thomas Molleson [1809-1876]
    159

Naylor, John, Mus. Doc......40, 152

Parker, *Rev.* Edwin Pond, D D.
    126, 127, 168, 169
Patton, Arthur 52

Pitts, W..........................82
Pratt, Waldo Selden
    18, 57, 158, 161, 167a, 184
Prout, Ebenezer.................106

Redhead, Richard ..24, 54, 87, 94, 116
Reed, Thomas German.............2
Reinagle, Alexander Robert [1799-1877]........................35
Robinson, John [1682-1762]........49
Russell, William, Mus. Bac. [1777-1813].........................60

Schlesinger, Sebastian B 69, 171
Scholefield, *Rev.* C. C...........21
Schumann, Robert, Ph. D.[1810-1856]
    86
Seymour, *Rev.* Edward.........165
Sheppard, *Rev.* Henry Fleetwood
    79
Smart, *Sir* Henry, Mus. Doc. [1812-1879] 36 (251), 84, 102, 216, 244, 256, 265
Smith, Samuel [1804-1873]
    20, 100, 101, 218
Spohr, Ludwig, Ph. D. [1784-1859]
    128
Stainer, John, Mus. Doc ..10, 11, 164
Steggall, Charles, Mus. Doc......194
Stewart, *Sir* Robert Prescott, Mus. Doc.........................3, 44, 115
Sullivan, *Sir* Arthur Seymour, Mus. Doc.........27, 41, 56, 135, 142, 175, 189, 212, 220, 223, 225, 257

Tours, Berthold 205
Tozer, A. E 48

Walch, J 213
Walker, F......................179
Warren, Samuel P 75, 85, 170, 181
Webb, George James............206
Webbe, Samuel, Jr. [1770-1843]..99
Weber, Carl Maria von [1786-1826]
    108
Wesley, Samuel Sebastian, Mus. Doc. [1810-1876].........96, 197
Westlake, Frederick 232
Wilcox, John Henry, Mus. Doc. [1827-1875]....................146
Willing, Charles Edward.... 61, 204
Willis, Richard Storrs 166
Wilson, Henry [1828-1878].........73

German.........7, 17, 19, 65, 76, 86, 93, 117, 119, 125, 192, 196, 221, 230, 235
French 214a
Italian 37
Portuguese 237
Hindoo 217
Anonymous (English)
    53, 62, 67, 90a, 120, 122, 141, 157, 207, 215, 229, 243, 252

Index of Tunes.

[INCLUDING ONLY THOSE THAT ARE KNOWN BY SPECIAL NAMES.]

Tune	No.	Tune	No.	Tune	No.
Adeste fideles	237	Ellerton	30	Packington	38
Aldersgate	186	Eventide	14	Paradise	224
Alford	219	Ewing	210	Passion Chorale	117
All Saints	221	Expectation	131	Pastor	146
Alleluia, dulce carmen	65			Pentecost	114
Almsgiving	178	Gloria in excelsis	64	Petrox	129
Alpha	148			Princethorpe	82
Alstone	61, 204	Hanover	70	Pretomartyr	191
Anfield	67	Happy Land	217		
Angel-Voices	41	Herald Angels	231	Regent Square	244
Arimathea	250	Hollingside	162	Resurrexit	257
Ascension	264	Holy Church	4	Rex Gloriae	265
Aurelia	197	Holy City	220	Rock of Ages	116
Austria	198	Holy Offerings	54	Ruth	101
		Holy Trinity	15		
Banstead	243	Honiton	59	St. Agnes	149
Beatitudo	226	Hursley	19	St. Ann's	63
Beechcroft	2	Hurstmonceux	106	St. Asaph	195
Belmont	99	Hymn to Joy	66	St. Basil	86
Ben Rhydding	35			St. Chad	94
Bentley	173	Irby	240	St. Clement	21
Berlin	76	Italian Hymn	37	St. Crispin	181
Bermondsey	207			St. Cuthbert	112
Bethany	256	Jazer	48	St. Cyprian	45
Birkenhead	215			St. Dionis	50
Bonn	230	Kirkstall	150	St. George's	104
Bromham	81			St. George's, Bolton	213
Budleigh	159	Lachrymae	135	St. Gertrude	189
		Lambeth	62	St. Hilda	125
Calvary	128	Lancashire	36, 251	St. Hubert	188
Canonbury	88	Langran	124	St. Leonard	23
Caritas	96	Langton	120	St. Lucian	56
Castle Rising	228	Laud	74	St. Mabyn	185
Childhood	47	Leila	203	St. Ninian	241
Chiselhurst	107	Leominster	229	St. Raphael	165
Christendom	259	Lilybourne	100	St. Sylvester	156
Christmas (Handel)	199	Litlington Tower	111	St. Ursula	232
Christmas (Matthews)	239	Lux Benigna	142a	St. Vincent	119
Cobham	42	Lux Eoi	223	Seymour	108
Come unto Me	174	Lux in tenebris	142	Stabat Mater	118
Credo	164	Lydney	53	Stephanos	167
		Lyons	71	Stoneleigh	29
Dawn	169	Lyra	52	Swabia	7
Day by Day	72				
Day of Praise	194	Maidstone	31	Temple	22
Day of Rest	143	Melita	105	Terry	25
Diademata	83	Missionary Hymn	208	Thanksgiving	43
Dix	235	Mistley	160	The Homeland	212
Dominus regit me	89	Morning Hymn	155	Treves	258
Duke St.	254	Mount Calvary	3		
		Muriel	55	Valete	27
Earlham	209			Verona	6a
Easter Hymn	252	New Calabar	121	Vox Angelica	176
Eden Grove	218	Newton Ferns	20		
Ein' feste Burg	196	Nicæa	58	Webb	206
Ellacombe	192	Nun danket	93	Wentworth	92
		O Quanta Qualia	214	Woodthorpe	26
		Oswald	130		

Index of First Lines.

ONE HUNDRED HYMNS WHOSE TUNES ARE COMPARATIVELY SHORT OR SIMPLE ARE MARKED THUS (*).

A mighty fortress is our God............. 196	Come, let us all unite and sing......... 170
Abide with me; fast falls the eventide... 14	Come, let us all with one accord....... 5
Above the clear, blue sky 42	Come, let us sing the song of songs .....* 254
Again, as evening's shadow falls.......* 25	Come, my soul, thou must be waking 11
All glory, laud, and honor.............. 75	Come, O Creator Spirit blest ....* 111
All hail the power of Jesus' name ......* 74	Come, Thou almighty King..............* 37
All my heart this night rejoices.......... 230	Come, Thou long-expected Jesus......... 131
Alleluia! Alleluia! Hearts to heaven ... 256	Come, Thou, O come 106
Alleluia! Sing to Jesus 77	Come unto Me, ye weary 174
"Alleluia!" Song of sweetness......... 65	Come, ye thankful people, come......... 104
Almighty God, Thy Word is cast.........* 47	Creator Spirit, by whose aid 105
Angels from the realms of glory......... 244	Crown Him with many crowns........... 83
Angel-voices, ever singing ....* 41	
Around Thy throne on high ....* 53	Day is dying in the west. 18
Art thou weary, art thou languid ....* 167	Dayspring of Eternity.................. 13
As helpless as a child 163	
As Mary knelt in tears..................* 122	Eternal Father, Thou hast said ....* 205
As with gladness men of old............* 235	Every morning mercies new 12
Awake, my soul, stretch every nerve..... 199	
	Faithful Shepherd, feed me.............* 141
Blessed Jesus, at Thy word.............. 32	Father, again in Jesus' name we meet..* 30
Blest Day of God, most calm, most......* 3	Father, hear Thy children's call ....* 138
Brief life is here our portion............. 212	Father, let me dedicate.................. 247
Bright was the guiding star.............* 243	Father of love, our Guide and Friend ...* 149
Brightest and best of the sons of the...... 241	Father of mercies, in Thy Word ....* 46
Brightly gleams our banner.............. 193	Father, whate'er of earthly bliss........* 134
	For all Thy care we bless Thee 95
Christ, above all glory seated...........* 72	For all Thy saints who from their labors 222
"Christ for the world" we sing ....* 207	For the beauty of the earth... 100
Christ is risen! Christ is risen 257	For thee, O dear, dear country.......... 213
"Christ the Lord is risen to-day"....... 252	"Forward!" be our watchword 216
Christ, whose glory fills the skies........ 6	From all Thy saints in warfare 218
Come, all ye faithful ....* 237	From Greenland's icy mountains 208
Come forth, O Christian brothers 36	
Come, gracious Spirit, heavenly Dove...* 113	Gentle Jesus, meek and mild ....* 121
Come, Holy Ghost, in love.............* 114	Glorious things of thee are spoken 198
Come, Holy Spirit, come ....* 107	Glory to Thee, my God, this night....... 28
Come, Jesus, Redeemer, abide Thou with 132	God, my King, Thy might confessing 98

INDEX OF FIRST LINES.—*Continued.*

God of my life, Thy boundless grace ...*	178
God, that madest earth and heaven	22
God the Father, be Thou near ....*	24
Golden harps are sounding	261
Good news on Christmas morning........	242
Gracious Father, hear our prayer	200
Gracious Saviour, gentle Shepherd.......	145
Gracious Spirit, dwell with me...........	110
Grant us, O our heavenly Father ....*	130
Hail the day that sees Him rise..........	264
Hail, Thou once-despised Jesus..........	85
Hail to the brightness of Zion's glad......	203
Hail to the Lord's Anointed..............	245
Happy are we, God's own little flock....	202
Hark, hark, my soul! Angelic songs are..	176
Hark, hark! the organ loudly peals	64
Hark! the herald angels sing	231
Hark, the sound of holy voices	223
Hark! what mean those holy voices......	234
Head of the Church triumphant..........	191
Holy, holy, holy! Lord God Almighty....	58
Holy, holy, holy Lord God of Hosts......	59
Holy night! peaceful night...............*	236
Holy offerings, rich and rare.............	54
Holy Saviour, we adore Thee	78
Holy Spirit, Truth divine...............*	108
I am trusting Thee, Lord Jesus.........*	168
I heard the voice of Jesus say............	175
I know no life divided	183
I lay my sins on Jesus	182
I lift my heart to Thee ....*	159
I think when I read that sweet story of old	246
I'm but a stranger here..................	225
In heavenly love abiding	172
It came upon the midnight clear.........	232
Jerusalem, my happy home..............*	215
Jerusalem on high	209
Jerusalem the glorious	211
Jerusalem the golden.....................	210
Jesus calls us o'er the tumult............*	185
Jesus Christ our Saviour	147
Jesus lives! Thy terrors now	255
Jesus, Lord, we kneel before Thee.......	123
Jesus, Lover of my soul	162
Jesus, my Lord, my God, my All.........	133
Jesus, Shepherd of the sheep ....*	181
Jesus, still lead on	188
Jesus, tender Shepherd, hear me........*	156
Jesus! the very thought is sweet ....*	88
Jesus, the very thought of Thee.........*	87
Jesus, we love to meet ....*	2
Joy fills our inmost heart to-day	238
Just as I am, without one plea..........*	180
Lamp of our feet, whereby we trace ....*	48
Lead, kindly Light, amid th' encircling ..	142
Lead us, heavenly Father, lead us	153
Look, ye saints, the sight is glorious	262
Lord, if on earth the thought of Thee ...*	226
Lord, in this Thy mercy's day ....*	135
Lord, it belongs not to my care ....*	151
Lord Jesus, when we stand afar	119
Lord, now we part in Thy blest name...*	52
Lord of all being, throned afar..........*	61
Lord, Thy Word abideth...............*	45
Lord, with glowing heart I'd praise Thee.	94
Love divine, all love excelling	136
My blessed Saviour, is Thy love ....*	184
My faith looks up to Thee	161
My God, how wonderful Thou art......*	62
My God, I thank Thee, who hast made..*	92
My God, is any hour so sweet..........*	40
My Saviour, be Thou near me........ ...	148
Near the cross was Mary weeping	118
Nearer, my God, to Thee	160
Night's shadows falling..................	17
No; not despairingly.....................	115
Now I have found a Friend	187
Now thank we all our God...............	93
Now the day is over.....................	16
Now to Him who loved us, gave us .....*	55
Now, when the dusky shades of night....	10
O cease, my wandering soul ....*	169
O Day of rest and gladness	4
O God, our Help in ages past............*	63
O God, the Rock of Ages	67
O holy Saviour, Friend unseen..........*	150
O Jesus, I have promised................	143

INDEX OF FIRST LINES.—*Continued*.

First Line	No.
O Jesus, Thou art standing	125
O Lord of heaven and earth and sea	*96
O Love Divine, that stooped to share	165
O One with God the Father	137
O Paradise! O Paradise	224
O sacred Head, now wounded	117
O Spirit of the living God	*204
O Thou, the contrite sinner's Friend	*157
O Thou, th' eternal Son of God	*249
O what the joy and the glory must be	214
O who like Thee, so calm, so bright	86
O Word of God Incarnate	44
O worship the King all-glorious above	70
O'er Bethlehem's hill, in days of old	233
Of Thy love some gracious token	56
On our way rejoicing	201
Once in royal David's city	*240
One sweetly solemn thought	229
Onward, Christian soldiers	189
Our blest Redeemer, ere He breathed	*112
Our Lord is risen from the dead	263
Out of the deep I call	120
Pleasant are Thy courts above	*31
Praise, my soul, the King of heaven	84
Praise the Lord, His glories show	68
Praise the Lord! Ye heavens, adore Him	66
Rock of Ages, cleft for me	*116
Safely through another week	*9
Saviour, again to Thy dear name	51
Saviour and Lord of all	*126
Saviour, blessed Saviour	*82
Saviour, breathe an evening blessing	*20
Saviour, like a shepherd lead us	*146
Saviour, teach me day by day	140
See, the Conqueror mounts in triumph	265
Sing Alleluia forth in duteous praise	220
Sing to the Lord a joyful song	97
Singing for Jesus, our Saviour and	81
So rest, my Rest	250
Soldiers of Christ, arise	*194
Sometimes a light surprises	173
Son of God, to Thee we bow	76
Songs of praise the angels sang	43
Spirit blest, who art adored	109
Stand up and bless the Lord	*35
Stand up, stand up for Jesus	*206
Star of morn and even	*127
Still, still with Thee, my God	*186
Summer suns are glowing	101
Sun of my soul, Thou Saviour dear	*19
Sweet is the work, O Lord	33
Sweet Saviour, bless us ere we go	27
Sweetly the birds are singing	*260
Ten thousand times ten thousand	219
The Church's one foundation	197
The dawn of God's new Sabbath	8
The Day of Resurrection	251
The day Thou gavest, Lord, is ended	21
The golden gates are lifted up	*258
The King of love my Shepherd is	*89
The Lord be with us as we bend	15
The morning bright, with rosy light	*155
The radiant morn hath passed away	26
The roseate hues of early dawn	228
The shadows of the evening hours	23
The Son of God goes forth to war	192
The strife is o'er, the battle done	259
There came a little Child to earth	*239
There is a green hill far away	*166
There is a happy land	*217
There's a Friend for little children	171
Thine for ever, God of love	*227
This Day, by Thy creating word	1
This is the Day of light	*7
Thou art gone up on high	152
Thou that once, by mother's knee	*154
Through good report and evil, Lord	*177
Through the day Thy love has spared us	29
Through the night of doubt and sorrow	195
Thy way, not mine, O Lord	*144
Thy Word is like a garden, Lord	*50
To Him who for our sins was slain	80
Uplift the banner! let it float	190
We praise, we bless Thee	69
We saw Thee not when Thou didst tread	164
Weary of earth, and laden with my sin	124
"Welcome, happy morning"	253
What grace, O Lord, and beauty shone	*128

INDEX OF FIRST LINES. — *Continued.*

When all Thy mercies, O my God	* 99	Who are these, like stars appearing	221
When, His salvation bringing	* 248	With joy we lift our eyes	* 38
When morning gilds the skies	79		
When the world is brightest	* 129	Ye servants of God, your Master	* 71

INDEX OF FIRST LINES OF CHANTS, ETC.

Alleluia! Amen ....[Response]	158	It is a good thing to give thanks	10
Amen ....[Response]	158	Make a joyful noise unto the Lord	39
Glory be to God on high	90	O all ye works of the Lord	73
Glory be to the Father	91	Our Father, who art in heaven	139
Holy! Holy! Holy ......[Sentence]	57	The Lord is my Shepherd	179
How amiable are Thy tabernacles	34	Thy Word is a lamp unto my feet	49
I will extol Thee, my God, O King	102	We praise Thee, O God	60

www.ingramcontent.com/pod-product-compliance
Lightning Source LLC
Chambersburg PA
CBHW032222230426
43666CB00033B/592